WAIT...NOW WHAT?

For you, From Bonnie Bing

Blue Cedar Press
Wichita, Kansas

Blue Cedar Press
PO Box 48715
Wichita, Kansas 67201

Visit the Blue Cedar Press website:
https://www.bluecedarpress.com

10 9 8 7 6 5 4 3 2 1
ISBN: 978-1-958728-42-0 (paperback)
ISBN: 978-1-958728-43-7 (ebook)

Cover art: Richard Crowson, former *Wichita Eagle* editorial cartoonist and freelance journalist
Cover design: Rod Pocowatchit, graphic designer, actor, film producer/director, and movie columnist for the *Wichita Eagle*.

Interior design: Gina Laiso, Integrita Productions
Editors: Gretchen Eick and Laura Tillem
Library of Congress Control Number: 2025945733

Printed in the United States of America

Praise for Bonnie Bing's book

"Pull back those heavy curtains and let Bonnie Bing's brilliant sunshine in! Bonnie will draw you along, in her conspiratorial manner, then, as she carries you through each column you will laugh out loud, maybe lapsing into a snort, but always nodding in agreement. Her writing simply radiates her happy outlook, as well as her kindness, inviting us to ride along with her as she ponders the small and larger issues; written as just-between-us-friends style, we willingly and eagerly comply, sharing her observations through her optimistic perspective on everything… this is not to say she's an obnoxious Pollyanna, but rather, a quirky commentator — a kinder and gentler Molly Ivins; our hometown, even wittier, Erma Bombeck."
~Annie Garvey
Community advocate and philanthropist

"Just finding a Bonnie Bing column in our Sunday paper gave my neediest moods a nice, warm upgrade. Who knew what was coming? Life on the home front? Nostalgia? Civility? Satire? Whatever the topic, her columns can make you feel, think, smile, laugh. This writer is special. Proof beckons!"
~Bob Getz
Former columnist for *The Wichita Eagle*

"Bonnie Bing is Wichita royalty (and not just because she plays the Fairytale Princess every year in Gridiron). Her writing is filled with insights into everyday life and her puckish sense of humor. Reading Bonnie's columns makes you feel like you're talking with an old friend."
~Tom Shine
Longtime journalist with *The Wichita Eagle* and KMUW radio

"Bonnie's columns have entertained me for 45 years. She is Wichita's Erma Bombeck. I'm one of her biggest fans becausd she makes me laugh out loud, cry, or just stop and ponder some of what life can throw at you. Get ready to feel all the emotions as you read these columns for the first or the tenth time."
~Ruthie Williams, longtime *Wichita Eagle* subscriber

"Reading one of Bonnie Bing's columns is like talking to a good friend — the kind who knows you so well, she says what you're thinking. She captures the wonder of everyday experiences and invites us to smile or shake our heads along with her. What a treat."
~Suzanne Perez
Assistant news director at KMUW

"In a meeting room on the Mezzanine at the old *Wichita Eagle* building, a seated crowd began to disintegrate into gaggles of lingering conversation when X-rated lyrics accidentally poured from the DJ's speakers.

The hackneyed phrase, 'I saw it happen in slow motion,' felt all too apt. Some of us who'd heard those lyrics before, froze as the bars unfolded. Then, that awful rap couplet dropped in the middle of this professional setting, and Bonnie Bing swept in. Like a hero.

'Oh, yes,' she said with effortless charm, 'we used to listen to that song in Sunday School.'

Laughter exploded in the room. The tension broke.

People consider her a socialite. Local royalty. But I came to see her as so much more.

She has beauty and charm, but those traits have made so many other people selfish, petty, and cruel.

Bonnie really cares. She's worked tirelessly in civic organizations and local charities. She's used her powers for good.

I've seen her comfort young women staffers. I've long suspected, given the women in my life, that the only thing harder than being a woman, was becoming one. And there would be Bonnie, uplifting someone. She wasn't Superwoman, but every bit a super woman.

You get this Bonnie in her book. You get the wit, the warmth, and the depth you may have overlooked because she really is so dazzling. You'd be hard-pressed to find someone who better embodied the best of Wichita and its layers of culture, than Bonnie Bing.

Who better to write about all of it than the heroine herself."

~Mark McCormick, New York Times Best Selling Author, former reporter at *The Wichita Eagle*, and inductee to the Kansas Newspaper Hall of Fame

"For decades Bonnie Bing advised Wichitans on fashion, beauty and culture. Her columns are sometimes humorous, sometimes touching, but always written with flair and affection for her hometown."

~Jean Hays, retired Editor at the *The Wichita Eagle*

"Bonnie is such a conversational writer that when you read her, you feel like you're sitting together on a cozy sofa while she spills the tea. Bon — as her close friends call her and you will, too, by the time you're done — is equal parts hilarious and poignant, all while being refreshingly real, just as she is in person."

~Carrie Rengers, reporter for *The Wichita Eagle*

Foreward

Back in 1997, I met Bonnie Bing during a job interview at *The Wichita Eagle* and decided she was the most glamorous person on earth. Her clothes were perfect. Her hair was perfect. Even her desk looked like it had been professionally decorated.

I was 26 years at the time, and Bonnie was… well, younger than I am as I type this. Having grown up in Dodge City, Kansas, I'd never encountered someone as put together as Bonnie. The only social columnists or fashion writers I was familiar with were the ones I'd seen on 1980s television shows – and they were all snooty, pretentious and quick to judge.

Bonnie, I was delighted to learn, was none of these things. She was warm. She was self-deprecating. She was friendly in a way that put me instantly at ease, and before my job interview ended, I felt like I'd known her my whole life. When I started at the paper a month later, Bonnie quickly became one of my closest friends, and that's never changed.

Of course, when I first met Bonnie, I didn't yet know what Wichita had already discovered from years of reading her columns in the paper: Despite her local celebrity and position of considerable influence, Bonnie was about as real as they came. Her observations about fashion, decorating, or just life in Wichita betrayed that, despite her blessings in the "taste" department, she was still just a girl from Wichita, a North High grad and proud Wichita State Shocker who had grown up dragging Douglas just like everybody else. People who read her columns related to her, and they could envision her winking mischievously as she typed.

Much of Wichita recognizes Bonnie from her time writing for *The Eagle*. Thousands of those people have actually met her. And hundreds of those people can count her as a friend. I'm positive that the people in Wichita who really know Bonnie would back me up on this: In real life, she comes across exactly as she does in her columns. Her writing voice and her actual voice are the same. She's authentic. She's kind. She's generous. She's surprisingly ornery, but in a classy way.

Bonnie also can be serious, and a line that *Wichita Eagle* photojournalist Jaime Green playfully penned in a tribute song played at Bonnie's retirement party in 2012 sums up this side of her pretty well: "She's traveled the world from Milan to New York, trying to help a Wichitan not look like a dork."

Bonnie's beloved mother, Louise, raised her daughter with a strong sense of propriety, and Bonnie has taken it upon herself to help the rest of us become a bit more civilized. When I know I'm going to see Bonnie, I try to at least accessorize. And I, for one, appreciate that Bonnie singlehandedly cured a generation of male *Eagle* journalists of their penchant for chewing on toothpicks after lunch.

Bonnie is one of Wichita's greatest treasures, and I'm grateful that decades worth of her charming, wise, relatable writing is now permanently preserved within the pages of this book.

By Denise Neil

A Happy Face
May 5, 1981

There are lots of ways to make a day a good day.

You can sing in your car on the way to work, count five things you're thankful for, tell yourself your favorite joke, or smile until you break into a genuine grin.

There also are ways to ruin a perfectly good day – like realizing a busload of people is watching you sing in your car, realizing all five things you're grateful for still aren't paid for, no longer thinking your favorite joke is funny, or forcing your smile until your teeth get dry, your lips nearly crack and your face aches.

But here is the absolute sure-fire way to ruin a perfectly good day: Try on swimsuits. Yep, that will turn a smile upside down in less than a minute.

It always seems incredible to me when I try on the first swimsuit of the new season (behind a locked dressing room door or a curtain held tightly shut with my hand) that I do later in the season, actually appear in public in something that exposes so much skin.

Mustering all my courage the other day I picked some little numbers from the racks and charged into the dressing room muttering to the saleswoman I would return when I was finished. In other words, no, DO NOT enter the dressing room saying, "Oh isn't that so cute on you" or "Come on out and let me see."

Well, I expected the green shiny one-piece to be a bomb but I didn't expect such a fall out. Long winter.

So, I tried the orange one-piece I had spotted in a fashion magazine. Not so bad but I could not bend over, and I doubt

I could survive sitting down in the thing. We should sue that magazine for false advertising. I didn't look a thing like the model in the picture.

After a traumatic half hour, I decided to stick with my old, faded (bless those stretched-out threads) bathing suits from years hence. As long as I stay wet, the old one looks new anyway.

My Special Dad
June 20, 1981

Father's Day and Mother's Day are my favorites, next to Valentine's Day. This day honoring fathers is probably special to me because I picked a special dad.

I got the dad who has given me at least $10,000 in unpaid $5 loans; the one who has a special wink he uses only on me. My dad is the one who never spanked me but gave me a talking to that I still remember, verbatim. My dad is the one who thinks I can do anything I set out to do and has made me believe that at least I can give it a heck of a try.

My dad is the one who does not roll his eyes heavenward and snicker while I explain one of my plans or schemes. He's also the one who left a board meeting to take a phone call from me, and taught me to ride my bike, He has magically put things into perspective when I was certain the end was near, and beckoned me with my entire name only when I was in a world of trouble.

My dad's the one I share many private jokes with and he has laughed out loud at every joke I've ever told him, even the ones I've made up (Now that's devotion). He's the one who waved to me every morning from the picture window as I drove off to high school, the one who, when I asked for a nickel, held out a handful of change. I'd take every cent, and he would let me. He has written checks to hospitals, piano teachers, several schools, beauty shops, car lots, doctors, clothing stores, Girl Scouts, greeting card companies (I just couldn't get all those cards sold), more clothing stores, dentists, and who knows what else - without a complaint.

I could go on, but instead why don't you take a few moments to consider the dad you picked out. If you get him a present, take time to get something he'll really like. If your pop chews Red Man or smokes Bull Durham, he won't be bowled over with a sterling silver monogrammed cigarette box, even if you wish he would be.

If he's one of those dads who thinks a necktie is a noose in disguise, don't give him a brand-new noose, even if you'd like to burn his favorite one with the hand-painted deer. Better yet, write him a poem, or just a couple of lines, especially from you.

But most importantly give him a loving hug, even if it has to be long distance, and tell him thanks.

Seventh graders were my favorite
August 28, 1981

Ah-h-h yes. The first week of school.

As a student, I loved the first week of school. Everything was so clean and new. It was a brand-new beginning.

As a junior high physical education teacher, I still loved the first week of school. (After I got over vacation withdrawal pains.) The gym floor polished to a high gloss, new equipment in the storeroom, new teachers in some of the rooms, and my favorite things, new students...seventh graders.

The shine on their faces matched the gym floor, and their eyes were the size of tennis balls as they went through the halls and toured the locker room.

It's no easy deal going from being the *big* sixth graders to being the *little* seventh graders. It seems a long time to the ninth grade when you're not sure you can make it to lunch time.

One mystery for our little partners starting junior high was the combination lock, and the first day of "dressing out" for physical education put me in a role much like a safe cracker. Those three numbers would be a complete puzzle to the person standing there in her gym suit, turning the dial. And you guessed it. The combination was written down on a piece of paper – inside the locker. Well, nobody is perfect for pity's sake.

Seventh graders also seem to lose their sense of direction. And, even if they don't, a ninth grader will help them by directing them the longest possible way to their next class.

I remember one little gal who, while sobbing into the soggiest Kleenex I had ever seen, told me she had decided to quit school. (It was only fourth hour!)

Then there was another seventh grader who was tiny for her age. She was so nervous the first day they showered that she charged into the shower with her tennis shoes and socks on.

Or the student who forgot her gym suit, so she wore her sister's that was three sizes too big. When she ran out to roll call, her shorts fell down around her knees, tripping her. She nearly broke her neck!

During the first week of school, most seventh graders feel that they will surely expire or at least have a nervous breakdown by Friday. Well, seventh graders, it's Friday, and you made it! It'll get easier every day, so there.

Oh, and if you're the mama or the papa of a seventh grader, you hang in there, too.

To live, to dance
September 20, 1981

My Joe Namath knees are killing me because my Martha Raye mouth blurted out that I was going to take a jazz dance class at Wichita State.

Once I said it and expounded on how badly I needed exercise, everyone in the LifeStyle department of the newsroom kept checking to see if I had enrolled.

The first class was not quite the catastrophe I expected, but close. When the teacher, Vicki Strawder, said, "Right foot, point your toes," my toes pointed all right but all in different directions. Four out of five cramped.

My toes got their act together about the time I thought I would die of thirst. I'm probably the oldest in class and was closet to cardiac arrest after 40 minutes of warmups. But I kept smiling. I wasn't about to let those young, leotard-clad, much younger dancers know I was worried about how I would get out of bed the next day.

When Vicki demonstrated, every step looked simple as pie. She seemed to float across the floor. But when it was my turn to cross the floor there was no floating going on.

As my tight old muscles warmed up I started feeling better and doing ok. The difference between my right and left came back. My heart pounded to the beat of the music so at least it wasn't audible to everyone in line as we waited our turn to cross the floor.

Maybe I saw "A Chorus Line," "Fame," and "All That Jazz" one too many times because I expected to be ready to audition after the first class. Wrong. At the rate I'm going I'll be ready at the age of 50.

I felt very stretched out and well exercised as I left class with my friend, Sue. We sort of leaned on each other and assured one another that next time wouldn't be so bad. Then we went in search of the largest limeade money could buy.

The next day as I walked around the newsroom trying not to limp, I was actually looking forward to the next class. At least that's what I told my co-workers.

To live is to dance...to dance is to ache...but it's worth it.

Flight of Fancy
October 6, 1981

Did Wilbur and Orville really know what they were doing?

The question ran through my mind recently on a plane trip from California. Airplanes should be called "the Wright Brothers Truth Cabins in the Air." I find it interesting that people pour out their hearts to perfect strangers on planes. Maybe those folks feel that strangers next to them thousands of feet in the air want to know their secrets, their frustrations and pour out every thought they've had for the past several weeks. Or years.

I usually end up sitting next to the perfect teller-venter-pourer. I am a "people person" (at least that's what I've been called from time to time), but I've often wished I could ride in the lavatory of the plane.

While in the sky, people have told me about problems with their spouses that should have been shared only with their spouses or a family counselor. Once, when I accidentally bumped the arm of the middle-aged male passenger next to me, I said, "excuse me." He said, "Oh, that's OK, it didn't hurt. Besides, things like that don't bother me anymore. I'm in analysis now." By the time we landed, I felt he owed me an analysis fee.

A ticket agent friend of mine said I attracted talkers because I got on the plane looking pleasant and smiling. So, I boarded flight No. 600 looking at the blue carpeting of the airplane and found my seat - right next to a little lady who resembled Jonathan Winters dressed up like an old lady. Bless her heart. Ah-h-h-h, at least no marital problems (her Harry died seven years ago).

But during the interrogation about everything I've ever done in my life, she learned I was at one time a junior high school teacher. For what seemed like a lifetime, I got to hear every detail of her granddaughter's learning disability and what she called "the present crumbling of the public educational system." She voiced all that while sucking down two vodkas on the rocks without batting an eye or missing a word. Maybe the answer is to sit down, fasten your seat belt and pretend to go into a coma, or at least a deep sleep. And, if you're next to a continuous chattering talking head who can't take a hint from your closed eyes, drool.

Boost Your Buddy Today
November 5, 1981

The holiday season, when you're supposed to take time to think of family and friends, is coming on at full speed. So, let's get a jump on it and concentrate on friends today because when we get neck deep in the season we won't have time to think of anything except making the December 25th deadline.

Just think of all the friendships that are famous and you'll realize having pals must be all right because folks for centuries have enjoyed having a buddy. For example, John Alden and Miles Standish, Lillian Hellman and Julia, Mickey Mouse and Donald Duck, Tom Sawyer and Huck Finn, Butch Cassidy and the Sundance Kid, Bob Hope and Bing Crosby, Katherine Hepburn and Spencer Tracy, Tonto and the Lone Ranger, Tom and Jerry.

Maybe you and your best friend aren't quite as well known as the above, but you're still important. That's why I declare this day, November 5th, to be Boost Your Buddy Day.

This is how you celebrate: Either call your best buddy on the phone (even if it is long distance) or write him or her a note (even if your buddy is right here in Wichita.)

Tell this person that even though you don't often say so, he or she is mighty important to you, and is one whose friendship you feel fortunate to share. You take it from there and add your own personal touch.

But I must warn you. At first, your friend will think you want a loan. When you turn down money, he or she will probably suspect you have an incurable illness and are calling everyone letting them know how much you care for them.

That's the best part, the fact that you took time just for your friend. No other reason.

If you haven't quit reading this by now, you're probably thinking: "Good grief, this idea must come from a middle-aged love child in a granny dress with a daisy stuck behind her ear, or someone who has overdosed on sensitivity training."

Wrong. (Well, except for the daisy.)

Just try it. I dare you! Do a little something today to boost your buddy and you'll both get a kick out of it.

If you get carried away, go ahead and send flowers or even tell the person face to face. (Now that's really celebrating with BYB Day.)

Well, don't just sit there! Get on the phone or get out your pen and paper. Who knows? You might get a call today yourself.

My License or My Life
December 10, 1981

The Scopes Monkey Trial, Brown vs. Board of Education, the Miranda Case, the Lindberg trial, the Nuremberg trials, the case of Emile Zola, Wichita Municipal Traffic Court - guess which one I was involved in. It wasn't exactly a scene from an old Perry Mason flick or right out of "And Justice for All," but it sure had enough excitement for this old girl. All of a sudden I thought perhaps I should have gone ahead and paid the ticket, but then I considered what it would be like to ride the bus all the time and a chauffeur would be too expensive. I was afraid my license was on the line, and as I raised my sweaty palm to be sworn in, I felt it was my life.

A matter of record I will admit (now) that my driving record stuffed in a folder in that office in Topeka is the thickness of a telephone book. Not New York's phone book, but maybe Wichita's. It seems I went through a few years where my right foot was uncontrollable and very heavy. But that ailment is gone and I've done better. Not perfect, but better.

One jag at traffic school was enough. And my car insurance resembles the national debt. So, there I was, having my day in court. The officer who issued the ticket was right there telling exactly what happened - complete with drawings on the chalkboard. And there was my attorney, defending me to the hilt.

Slightly exaggerated, but I did feel we had a good argument and by using my judgment of not obeying the "right turn only" sign I had saved lives.

I found myself hoping the judge had had a good breakfast and a pleasant morning. His Honor heard both sides. He listened as closely as if my life depended on it (little did he know) and read out of a big book (bigger than the New York phone book). The prosecuting attorney said he believed I was totally guilty.

Darn him. But I thought he'd say that. Then the judge, who has my undying gratitude (and vote, if he ever needs it), let loose with two minutes of legal jargon that meant my friends didn't need to bake a cake with a file in it and I wouldn't be hitchhiking back to work. My faith in the judicial system is truly restored. Even if we had lost in court, I think I would have felt better just knowing I got to tell my side of the story. So, if you're behind a white Mustang driving along obeying every traffic sign in sight, just honk, wave and go around because I'm not speeding. For now.

How an Insight Turned a Gift into a Treasure
December 23, 1981

I was on hall duty, paying my debt to society as a junior high teacher, and looking forward to Christmas vacation just as much as the kids were.

A seventh grader rushed up to me, as she did every day, to say good morning and sometimes give a long explanation of why she forgot her gym suit. But one morning she showed me a pin her grandmother had given her that weekend.

It wasn't 14 karat gold by any means, and several of the stones were missing. "Grandma said somebody at the church gave it to her at her Sunday school gift exchange, and she gave it to me because some of the stones fell out," she told me looking down at the pin. "I don't think they're real stones," she said.

I told her they were just as pretty as real rubies and diamonds and the pearl in the center looked authentic to me. She couldn't have been prouder. So proud when she ran out for roll call, she had it pinned on her gym suit.

I told her I'd keep it for her so she wouldn't lose it or stab herself if the catch came undone. After class, as I handed it back to her, I noticed the pearl was missing. We found it in my pocket and glued it back on the pin with Elmer's glue.

As she left the building that afternoon, I noticed she had taken the pin from her dress and put it on her coat. That night she probably pinned it on her pajamas. Every day for the next two weeks she wore her prize possession and twice I had to break out the glue to put the pearl back. (It was beginning to look a bit crusty.)

The last day of school before Christmas break the three o'clock bell rang and students stampeded past yelling "Merry

Christmas!" After the building cleared in record breaking time, I went into my tiny office thinking of sleeping late the next morning and my mom's cooking.

In the middle of my desk was a small package wrapped in notebook paper and pale green ribbon that had been used many times before. There was a rule that teachers were not to accept gifts from students, but my curiosity got the best of me.

The box was made from the bottom part of a kitchen match box and the gift was wrapped in a Kleenex.

It was the pin.

We're still here
March 11, 1982

Whew! Thank goodness you're here to read this. Jupiter and its planet partners didn't do us all in.

Stargazers John Gribbin and Stephen Plagemann were wrong when they stated in their book, *The Jupiter Effect*, that Wednesday of this week nine planets would line up and cause a heck of a mess – that the whole world as we know it was going to bite the dust, or at least California would slide into the ocean. Boy, would I have been hacked because I'm going to California in 10 days.

Last week I asked a few folks just what they would have done if they'd truly believed John and Steve's prediction of Goodbye World Day.

One 40-year-old single mother said she'd do everything she wanted to so she'd be so tired it wouldn't matter.

A 67-year-old man said, "I'd eat a big, wonderful meal with heavenly music playing in the background.

A 39-year-old mother of two said she knew what she wouldn't do. "I would not go buy another bathing suit. I'd just wear my old one."

A 50-year-old man said, "I'd get busy and take up painting. . . nude women."

Another man said he'd play havoc with his American Express charge card.

I decided I'd go buy the most beautiful dress I've ever seen. It's a $3,000 bugle-beaded evening gown by Akira. Might as well go out in style.

Not many of us relish the idea of the world coming to an end. A couple of people said, "Well all our worries would be over."

True. I guess we wouldn't have to worry about what old John Gribbin and Stephen Plagemann will predict next.

Bonne as Gumby

Work with big star is a hot time
July 11, 1989

It was tough to decide if it was an all-time high point, or was it a low? It was, after all, a chance to perform with a well-known star. But should a grown woman really put on a Gumby costume, run out on a baseball field and tackle The Famous Chicken? Ted Giannoulas is the 34-year-old man who calls himself "a sports promoter," he said, because if he says he's a chicken people think he means cowardly. He said he earns "six figures easily in a good year" traveling 250 days a year. Before Saturday's Wrangler game, I met Giannoulas in the locker room at Lawrence-Dumont Stadium.

The dynamic chicken talks with more animation than a cartoon character and as much enthusiasm as a high school cheerleader. "OK, OK, this is going to be great. I've got a new routine just for you. I forgot to bring your costume, but somebody went after it and they'll be right back. Right now we'll go over what you're going to do. You'll be great as Gumby, this is going to be so much fun," the 5-foot-4-inch Giannoulas said, waving his arms around, looking me over head to toe and never drawing a breath.

A great Gumby, huh? As he rattled off the choreography behind the routine that "the crowd was going to love," his dark brown eyes flashed. "OK, when Cookie (the Wrangler mascot) tries to race a little kid around the bases, he's going to pretend to come up lame. I'll take the lead, and I'll be ahead of the little kid, so you're going to tackle me SO he can win. Now, we'll do this in the middle of the fifth inning. You'll wait right here and my assistant will tell you when to come running out.

27

"Catch me between third and home and just jump on me, pounce on me, whatever, just tackle me however you want, wave the little kid on to home and he'll win, and Gumby has saved the day!"

As he talked, he was seeing the whole skit flash before his eyes. I was seeing my humiliated husband in the stands if word leaked out that Gumby, who just tackled The Chicken, was his wife. Even so, listening to this guy was like taking an upper. No wonder he makes a ton of money running around the country spreading humor and enthusiasm. I was anxious to get on with the show.

But since it was 90 degrees and very humid I wasn't terribly anxious to put on the green Gumby suit lined with foam rubber. Besides, it was tough to see out of.

But Giannoulas was going to be on the field for most of the game. "I go out in the middle of the second. Even Frank Sinatra needs a warmup," he said, grinning. The three Chicken outfits he wears during one game were hung in the locker room, positioned for quick changes. A huge fan circulated hot air, but the heat didn't seem to bother his operations manager, Al Silva.

"At least it's not raining," he said with a smile spreading under his thick moustache. "If a game is rained out, I don't get paid." After explaining how to don the Gumby suit, he said, "Come back down here at the top of the fourth so you'll have plenty of time." Oh dear. What I didn't want was time to think about being Gumby. A sellout crowd of 8,000 started pouring through the gates. During the second inning, The Famous Chicken made his first appearance and fans applauded, shouted, screamed and waved.

They giggled and cheered. As the Chicken saluted, Andy lead the crowd in clapping, scratched under his tail feathers, and generally acted goofy. At the top of the fourth inning, I headed back to the locker room wondering if the kid selling cold drinks had ever wanted to be Gumby. And if he hadn't, how much he would take to be a stand-in. Silva pulled the head and the rest of the Chicken outfit off a sopping wet Giannoulas.

Wearing only a sweaty yellow stretch body suit and his webbed feet, Giannoulas gulped down Gatorade, grinned at me and said, "Gumby, we'll knock 'em dead." I was handed a long, green costume packed full of foam rubber to form Gumby's thick legs and a shirt with hands sewn onto the sleeves. I was relieved that my tennis shoes went completely through the legs. Running was going to be tough enough, but at least my feet were going to be on the ground ... until the tackle. Once the bit started, action was fast.

Cookie ran and faked the injury. Al yelled, "Go now!" The Chicken was nearing home, so Gumby needed to put on some steam. I grabbed him. Not seeing anything but the inside of the costume, I fell to the ground. Lucky for me The Chicken was under me.

It's a wonder it didn't kill him, or at least break a wing. I sat on The Chicken while he stretched his arm to reach home plate. He was yelling, "Wave him in, you're doing great!" The little guy who ran the bases ran past to home. I danced around like Rocky and wiggled my rear at The Chicken. I wondered if that was something Gumby would do.

Then I tried to see to get to the dugout. Finally I found Silva, and he helped me negotiate the steps. Well, shoot. It was over too fast. That was so fun, and since nobody knew who I was, I wanted to go back out and dance with The Chicken or something.

Instead, I stepped out of the Gumby outfit, glad to feel the air. My T-shirt was soaked with perspiration. Not a glamorous job. It wasn't long before Giannoulas came through the door, taking off the Chicken head. "You were great, they loved it!" he said.

"Great," was certainly an exaggeration, but it was nice to hear. At the top of the eighth inning The Famous Chicken autographed color photographs. "Hi, little pork chop. Give me five. Is this for your brother? That's nice of you. Are you going to sell it to your brother? Bye, bye, eat pizza, not chicken."

Brett Williams, 6, waiting his turn in the line of 200 said, "He's funny, Dad." He is funny ... with or without Gumby.

Unfamiliar Ground
February 3, 1983

NOTE: Steve Doocy who is now on FOX News now was on KAKE TV here in Wichita in the early 80s. He also was in the cast of Gridiron. Steve is a very funny and very nice guy. The story we did was about favorite restaurants. The other three women in the story chose very fancy restaurants. I chose NuWay.

Let it be known right now that all media are not the same. When you're on television, you have to worry about your makeup, your hair, your clothes and whether or not you can complete a sentence. When you write for a newspaper, nobody pays any attention to your lipstick, your hair, or your clothes.

Editors do believe, however, in complete sentences. I know about both because I recently was Steve Doocy's co-host on the "P.M. Magazine" to be broadcast Feb. 16. I don't want to give the format of the show away, but I will tell you what it was like being taped for the telly - it was fun but not easy.

Thank goodness for cameraman Bill Hernandez, my source of encouragement. Funny how he could do about 100 things at once and keep telling me I was doing fine. "One-take Bonnie," he called me. Optimistic fellow, Hernandez. Producer Nancy Wells told me which direction to look and tried to keep Doocy in line.

Impossible. The taping involved eating out at a local restaurant. One thing about television, it draws a crowd. There's something about loads of equipment and 10,000-watt bulbs making everything as bright as daylight that will distract your average diner. There's always a distracting crowd in the newsroom, of course, but most of us work here.

Nobody pays any attention to anyone else unless you bring in food. We were eating during part of the show. It's bad enough going to lunch with people you don't know well, but worse to invade strangers' television screens at dinner time, script in one hand, napkin in the other. I kept dropping things. The battery attached to my back and the microphone clipped to my front made me feel a teensy bit like the bionic woman.

Once the battery came loose and skidded all the way down my back to the ground. It felt exactly like a very large ice cube and made me forget my name. Take two. All this time I was worrying about my tendrils straightening and my nose looking like it was coated with Crisco. Did the dark circles under my eyes make this look like an episode of "Rocky Raccoon Goes to Lunch"? But then it was time to worry about words, too.

Good grief! Here in the newsroom, you can kick your shoes off under your desk and nobody knows, unless some semi funny sportswriter hides a shoe. And behind my computer screen, I can squeeze my eyes shut and think of a word or spelling before committing myself to type. While I didn't have to worry about spelling on television, I did have to pronounce words correctly. I guess it's a trade-off. If all this sounds exaggerated ...well, you try it.

Television is exciting, though - so exciting my toes curled every time it was my turn to say something. But then my toes curl every time I read one of my rough drafts.

When it comes to swimwear, the devil's in the details
April 30, 2001

Spring arrived, but for a while there was still a chill in the air. Oh sure, some people are chomping at the bit to have warm, even hot, weather so they can don fewer clothes and jump into various bodies of water.

With the prospect of putting on a swimsuit, I wouldn't mind if a snowflake hit me on the head at this very moment.

Nope, not kidding.

After looking through a mountain of photos featuring smooth-skinned, flat-bellied models and writing about the latest trends in swim wear, I decided to take the bull by the horns, grit my teeth, and go purchase a new swimsuit.

Once in the car, I reminded myself that those perfect bodies in the photos - the ones with no cellulite, no varicose veins, no pasty white hue - may have been airbrushed, so I shouldn't use them as a standard. Besides, none of them is older than 20, and gravity will catch up with them.

The first stop on this dreaded trek was the last.

Yes, the colors were bright, the styles and trims dazzling, and the choice extensive.

I chose black, no trim, industrial-strength fabric. I have yet to have it on. No, I didn't even try it on in the store, and yes, I understand I can't take it back. I went without breakfast and had very little for lunch, thinking by midafternoon I'd feel like it was a "thin day" and I could bear to bare it.

I couldn't.

It doesn't help that I always run into a half dozen people who know that I feel swim wear is designed by Satan himself. Before I knew it, two salespeople and three shoppers were giving me

33

their opinions on which one to try on. I kept thinking they'd go concentrate on what they were in the store for, but noooooo.

One woman, bless her heart, was under the impression I would go in the dressing room, put the swimsuit on, and come out to the "big mirror" so I could see the suit better and the group could see.

The chances of that happening were the same as they would be of my streaking the mall and doing a cartwheel-round-off at the exit. It ain't gonna happen, honey.

After looking at no fewer than 10 swimsuits, I just sort of vapor locked and ended up shoving the plain, black suit at the salesperson and muttering "This one is fine. I'll take it."

She was surprised, the shoppers/opinion-givers were surprised. Heck, I was surprised, but I wanted out of there.

At least when it's time to face the music, or in this case the screech, I won't be in a dressing room the size of a shoe box, struggling, huffing, cussing, and puffing with a sweat mustache and red face.

Once I got home, I threw the new suit in the drawer with two old swimsuits, and I swear I heard them talking and laughing about the misery they cause.

Ha! I'll punish them all and leave them in the drawer all summer. . . . Let it snow, let it snow, let it snow.

Roles Reversed - Now it's time for me to take care of Mom
August 2, 2010

NOTE: When this column ran in the paper I got more than 100 emails, notes in the mail and phone calls. The response surprised me. I was glad I wrote it.

Bonnie and her Mom Louise

The blue-and-white Kleenex flower said it all. It was part of a Mother's Day card I made Mom in second grade, a mere 57 years ago. My brother and I discovered it recently as we took a difficult but pleasurable trip down memory lane, going through my mother's belongings in the house she had lived in since the mid-'50s. Mom, who now lives at the Masonic Home, didn't throw away anything with sentimental value. Or even things with no sentimental value.

As I sniffed the flattened Kleenex flower (I had, after all, dabbed perfume on it), my brother asked me about it. I told him I made it for Mom when I was in Miss Noblett's class at Alcott Elementary School. Everyone in the class made similar flowers, attaching them to Mother's Day cards using pipe cleaner stems. I had a wreck on my bicycle on the way home and the flower became detached, which worried me more than my skinned knee. Mom said she liked it that way, put it in a jelly glass and displayed it in the kitchen for a couple of weeks. When one day it was gone, I figured she had thrown it away.

But all these years later, I discovered otherwise. The day we moved Mom out of her house was one of the most difficult days of my life. We moved a few pieces of furniture to her new residence, prompting her to say optimistically that her stay at the Masonic Home was probably temporary and she'd be back home before long. Chicken that I am, I couldn't tell her the chances of that were slim. Before her bed was moved, she and I lay down on it to talk things over, just as we had done a million times before. I felt bad for her but knew it was a move that had to be made. And I felt sorry for myself because I knew I'd no longer come through that back door yelling, "Mom."

For those of us blessed with a happy childhood, there is a wonderful familiarity with the house where we grew up. It proves to be a safe, comfortable place no matter how old we are. It's always home. Many of my friends had told me how tough it is to move a parent or parents out of a house they've lived in so long, a place that's almost an extension of them. But for their health and safety, it's sometimes necessary. That's when you know you're amid role reversal.

They say there's no manual for parenthood. Well, there is no manual for adult children dealing with aging parents. Yes, there are thousands of books written, but read what you will, there is still a feeling of being unprepared. And that catches most of us by surprise. My mom put up with a lot, whether it was making a dress for me for Glee Club at the very last minute or waiting on me hand and foot when I had a broken leg. She did mom duty better than June Cleaver, although she didn't wear pearls and heels while running the sweeper. And now it's my turn.

As I looked through old photos at her house that day, I realized something that made me smile. I will take care of my mom for the rest of her life, but it will never be equal to all she has done for me. One thing is certain: I'm going to make her a new and fragrant Kleenex flower.

Death of a wonderful mother at year's end leaves a hole in the heart
Januaary 12, 2014

Little did I know on Dec. 23 when I wrote about not making resolutions for the new year but taking a moment to look back at personal and very specific events of the past year, that for me both would be so evident. Our trip to France was probably the most fun time I had in 2013, but the most difficult thing that happened was not just a tough way to end 2013 but perhaps the most difficult thing I've ever faced. My mom passed away Dec. 28.

She was in the hospital, but it was still a shock. She was probably ready to leave this world, but it has put a hole in my heart. No one will ever love me the way my mom did. So many people have been so kind and supportive, there is no way to thank them. I do know I haven't felt nearly sorry enough for my friends and family who lost their moms.

My brother, Dale, says he feels the same way. We're both grateful for the many, many wonderful memories of our outstanding mom. I was very upset when I realized my mom died alone. No one was in the room. My friend Sally Thompson explained that was the way Mom wanted it.

"She would have hung on and hung on if you had been sitting there," she said. That might be true because Mom waited to take her last breath until the nurse had left the room to get a warm blanket.

Tom Shine is one of my *Eagle* co-workers I've missed the most since I retired. I will never forget what he said after the funeral. "So much of what I heard about your mom reminded me of you. It is difficult to lose those who have shaped us, but your mom isn't really gone because her wonderful qualities live in you," he said.

I do hope I have some of her qualities because I admired her and so did many others. My dad died 10 years ago, and that was heartbreaking, but this experience is like nothing I've ever gone through. "It's different when it's your mom," my cousin Garry Hoy said. "And it's different when you lose your last parent." So many people have given me good advice.

I've read the cards and e-mails several times because it makes me realize how many people also had great moms and they assure me, "It gets better." Those of us who grew up in a loving home knowing our parents' main concern was our health, safety and comfort are the fortunate ones. Roles may be reversed when parents are elderly, but their unconditional love remains long as they live. I'll miss that. And I'll miss my mom's humor, her wisdom, her generosity and the best smile I've ever seen.

Sibling's Day an opportunity for us to celebrate sisters, brothers
May 9, 2014

Happy Mother's Day. Quite frankly I'll be glad when it's over and the displays and ads featuring moms are gone. Not meaning to sound grouchy or sorry for myself, but I'm both. This is the first Mother's Day I haven't had my mom to celebrate.

Once you reach adulthood you realize that even though their personalities are "larger than life" and they seemed like "people who would live forever." Your parents, yes, YOUR parents, would die someday. And regardless of how old you are, when both parents are gone, you feel like an orphan. Thank goodness for family, especially if you're lucky enough to have a sibling.

That's why I think we should have a new day to celebrate. Sibling's Day. We have everything from Father's Day to Grandparent's Day to Groundhog Day to Administrative Assistant's Day. Let's celebrate our brothers and sisters. If you don't have any, substitute a cousin or someone who is as close as a sibling.

Today I'm letting my little brother, Dale, know I love and appreciate him and I couldn't have gotten through the loss of our parents without him. He's my only sibling because we suffered the loss of our 16-year-old brother when we were kids. Siblings are an important part of life and, even if you fought like cats and dogs when you were kids, and maybe you still do, wouldn't it be nice to put any hurt feeling, jealousy, and grudge away for one day and express your love?

It hurts my heart when I hear siblings fighting, regardless of age. I think the last time Dale and I were mad at each other was more than 20 years ago. Or at least mad enough to react. He may have a different story, but that's the last time I remember. When a friend of mine said, "I wish my brother would move to the edge of the earth and fall off," I wanted to shake her until her teeth rattled. Instead, I told her to talk to him and try to work things out because she had only one brother, her only sibling. Then I asked her how she'd feel if something did happen to him.

When I suggested Sibling's Day to another friend, she thought it was a good idea, but an acquaintance said, "I guess it's a good idea, but. I don't have anything in common with my brother or my sister, so I'd probably not do anything." I had to laugh because she has parents in common. Besides, what does that have to do with anything?

My brother and I don't have the same interests. He's a marathon runner (Boston and New York Marathons this year), he's a triathlete and an Iron Man. He is a scuba diver and would live on a boat if at all possible. Needless to say, I am none of the above.

He is methodical, organized, a border-line neat freak and knows a whole lot about insurance. Once again, none of the above.

What we do have in common are great memories, funny stories only he and I can appreciate fully, and loved ones. He got married very young and is still married to the same terrific woman, Peggy, who I think of as a sister. Their daughter Amy is and always will be a special person in my life, as will Eric, their son. I'm so proud of both of them. And I have Dale to thank for bringing these people into my life.

It's a great day to honor moms, stepmoms, and yes, mothers-in-law. Honor all of them, even those who aren't with us anymore.

This, or any day actually, is a good time to let your siblings know you love them and appreciate their love and support. Besides, it will make your mama happy.

Celebrating the bond between grandparents and grandchildren
September 13, 2015

Today is Grandparent's Day. Some might say it's just another day that is declared this or that so the greeting card companies can make money. But there are those of us who love days designated for moms or dads, siblings, teachers, doctors, and, yes, grandparents.

One of the best things in my life is being a grandma. Technically, I'm a step-grandma, but when I used that term once, all three granddaughters told me to never say it again. If you're a grandparent, you may or may not get a "Happy Grandparent's Day" greeting today, but take a minute to think about your role. Think about your grandparents.

I'm so different than either one of my grandmothers. I was closest to my mom's mom. We called her Granny. She was an energetic, funny woman who wore her gray hair in a braided bun. She lived in Latham, Ks. on the corner of the main drag across from the Methodist church and next door to the Baptist church. If you wanted to get into either church, the keys were hanging on Granny's front porch on a big nail. That amazed me. Anyone could get into the churches.

I asked if they were worried someone would get the key, go in and steal something. Granny huffed and informed me there was nothing in either church worth stealing.

Grandpa had a heart attack around the age of 60 and couldn't do much from then on. He played solitaire by the hour, and he and I would play hearts. Anytime I see someone playing solitaire, I think of him. I'm still no good at hearts.

Granny instilled in me the notion that you simply do what needs to be done. Sometimes it's not easy, but just get to it. She took in laundry. In the summer, when we would stay with them. She'd get up at 4 a.m. so she could get the washing and ironing done before it got too hot. She never complained and didn't seem to think that ungodly hour was any big deal. To this day grape Kool-Aid, porch swings, geraniums, and the smell of freshly ironed clothes make me think of my Granny.

My other grandparents lived down the road on the next corner on the other side of the street. My dad's parents had 12 children. I learned from that grandmother that I didn't want to have 12 children.

Grandma always looked very tired and seemed completely worn out. And who wouldn't be? Grandpa Bing couldn't hear, but he was a funny old guy. They both seemed much older than they actually were.

When I was getting my hair cut Tuesday (oh, all right, and colored), I asked my hairdresser Melissa Tinker about her grandparents. She has only one grandparent left, her grandpa. "I really do miss my grandmas," she said. Melissa has four children and says she's so glad they have two grandmas. "And it's great that they are so different. The kids get two completely different experiences when they are with their grandmas," she said. "At my mom's house, there are lots of kids, cousins and it's wild and chaotic, just like it was when I was a kid at my grandma's house. At Mary Lou's (her husband's mom), it's calm, quiet and there is more opportunity for one-on-one time." Melissa summed it up by saying, "Grandparents are the best. It takes a village."

I also chatted with Tasha Thrash, who seemed wise beyond her 21 years. She says she is from a close-knit family and knows the importance of staying in touch. "I think I talk to my grandparents more than most people my age. I talk to them probably once a week," she said. When I asked her if she has learned anything from her grandparents, she said without hesitation, "My parents are divorced, but I learned what a relationship should look like from my grandparents. They were married for 59 years before my grandpa died of cancer." Tasha says she learned a valuable lesson seeing their relationship.

If you're a grandparent, make memories with those grandchildren and recall the ones you've already made. Think of the memories you made with your grandparents. If you're a grandchild, call your grandparents. You'll make their day. Because it is, after all, Grandparent's Day.

Holidays are about memories and traditions
December 23, 2018

The holiday season brings out the best in all of us. Oh, all right maybe not ALL of us. But being an observer of the human race I've decided I know the problem for those who say they hate the holidays. Stress.

True, nobody enjoys stress, but those who concentrate on perfection are the ones who end up in a meltdown worse than Frosty's.

Let's be real. We're not taking part in a Hallmark movie here, folks. We're just trying to get blended families to blend, make gravy with no lumps, and prevent toddlers from tipping over the tree. Oh, and to make sure no one was left off the gift list.

That last one brings back a funny memory. I remember getting a familiar looking vase from a friend. It was in a gift bag, and the vase still had a bit of water in the bottom! I had given the vase to her a couple of years earlier. I noticed it had been filled with flowers before the gift exchange started. I gave it back to her the next year but at least I dried it out first.

But the holidays should be about two things. Memories and traditions. If you have those, every holiday season will be a time you look forward to.

From the time I was in the third grade until the year before my dad died at age 90, he and I went shopping for my mom's Christmas gift. Those traditional excursions have provided me with some very fun and fond memories.

Dale, my younger brother, as he is quick to point out, and I have a tradition of going to Latham every December. It is 50 miles east and 10 miles south of Wichita. We put wreaths on our mom, dad and brother's graves.

I look forward to a few hours with my only sibling reminiscing about our many relatives who lived in the little town. We went this week and just as every year there was laughter and tears.

Now the town is mostly abandoned, which makes us sad. As we drove by Granny's house, I realized Dale is now the only person who can share memories of summers and holidays in Latham.

We talked about our best Christmases and our worst. It was easy to remember the worst for both of us. It was the year our 16-year-old brother was gravely ill with cancer. He was lying in a hospital bed that was in our parent's bedroom. They didn't leave his side.

On Christmas Mom told Dale and me we could go open presents if we wanted to. He and I sat on the living room floor by ourselves. "I got a tractor, and I remember it was wrapped in a big Kleenex box. I still have that tractor," he said.

I remember being shocked when I unwrapped the fluffy pair of red slippers I had seen at Innes department store. My friend's grandmother worked there and made arrangements for me to receive them because my mom couldn't shop much that year.

Dale said his best Christmas was when their daughter Amy got engaged. It didn't surprise me to hear my exuberant niece jumped on her fiancé when he was down on one knee. "She nearly broke his leg," Dale said laughing.

I've simply had too many wonderful Christmases to choose a favorite.

As we chatted about the holidays in general, we agreed the best part of the season is that you are happily forced to have down time with family and friends.

Forget perfection. Cherish the time when work and worries are stored away while you make memories with people you love.

Now that's a gift.

Today is a good day to stop and think of your mother
May 5, 2016

Last week some people on NPR were talking about the importance of play. The conversation brought to mind how my mom used to say, "Go play." She would say this to me and my brothers when we were under foot or bickering with each other. Those thoughts brought back several memories of my mom and made me take note that today is Mother's Day.

Yes, it is Mother's Day. Call it a commercial holiday or whatever, but this is a good opportunity to stop what you're doing and think of your mom. These days we don't stop enough. And we don't think enough about the people who have played a major part in our lives.

I realize everyone was not as lucky as me. I had an A+, number one mom. But even if you didn't, you're here because of her so give her a minute or two of brain time.

When I suggested this to a friend, she said, "Oh I'll be thinking about her all right, I'm taking her to brunch." Yes, that can be part of it, spending time is a great gift, but it's the perfect day to *think* about your mom.

Here, this will make it easy:

First, ask yourself "What is the most important lesson I learned from mom?" One friend made sort of a snorting noise and said, "She taught me that I would never be the type of mother she has been." Well, ok, that's a lesson, but thankfully there are those of us with a more positive viewpoint.

My mom taught me to smile, and a compliment is better than a frown and a sharp tongue. And she always seemed to be able to look at the other person's point of view. I continue to work on that.

Now, think about a time when you laughed with your mom and the instance still makes you smile when you recall it. I have a lot of those, but a favorite was when Mom and I were shopping for swimsuits at Innes Department Store and we were laughing so hard we were crying. I think the saleslady thought we had had several cocktails with lunch. She kept asking us if we were all right, which made us laugh more.

Also, think of something your mother doesn't know about you, or perhaps something you think you got away with. If you're lucky enough to still have your mom, think about telling her this little secret sometime. Not long before she passed away, I told Mom some things I thought she didn't know. Not a single one surprised her and she already knew most of them. I was the one who was surprised.

And one more thing: Think of something your mom did for you that helped you succeed, or maybe she "saved your bacon," made a bad situation better, or simply solved a problem. My list of those is very, very long.

If you've read this, I bet you've thought of your mom. That's good because think of the amount of her time spent thinking about you.

Happy Mother's Day.

Dad knew the secret to a long life
June 26, 2015

My dad has been gone now for more than a decade, but once again Father's Day brought back memories of that special day we used to celebrate with him.

It was around Father's Day that my family and many of my friends anxiously awaited Dad's tomato crop to start ripening. He grew the best tomatoes ever. By July 4 we could start pulling a few off the vines. He grew other vegetables, but those tomatoes were the best. He constantly read how to improve his crop. He had the soil tested then he would add this or that to enrich the soil. After fertilizing his garden, I remember how happy Dad was when their backyard smelled like a barnyard. Mom, well, not so much.

Maybe because he was forced to quit school so young to work on his parents' farm, he had a quest for learning all his life. One of 12 children, he was determined not to go into farming, to live in a city and do well in the business world. And he did. But he never stopped learning.

When my parents traveled Dad would read about where they were going before they left. When I was in grade school we got a set of encyclopedias. I was mystified that Dad read those for fun.

At the age of about 80 he taught himself to play his dad's fiddle. I was at work in the newsroom one day when Dad called and said, "Bon, it's your old man, got a minute? Okay, are you ready? "He put the phone down and played "Turkey in the Straw" on his dad's fiddle, then picked up the phone. "Could you tell what song it was?" he asked. I assured him it was easy to tell it was "Turkey in the Straw." Then I asked for an encore, and he laughed because so far that was the extent of his repertoire on that particular instrument.

I remember thinking how great it was that he was still wanting to learn new things. It seems every book or article written about how to stay healthy as you age advises using your brain by learning new things. And staying as physically active as possible.

I have no doubt that's why Dad was moving and grooving until the day he died at age 90 while working in his garden.

Along with the craziness, some really good things happened in 2019
January 5, 2020

NOTE: Little did we know what was coming next – Covid!

Wouldn't you know it, just when I was finally writing the correct year on my checks, it's time to put 2020 on that line. How can that be? When you're a child it is eons between when birthdays and Christmas roll around. It seemed celebrations rode on the back of an old turtle.

But get a few years on you and before you know it, you're saying what your parents always said, "Time flies and the older you get the faster it flies." But it's like the weather: There's not a darned thing we can do about it. So, let's just rock on and make 2020 a year we'll look back on and smile, feel proud, grateful and happy. Too much? All right, pick two of those.

For the past few years on New Year's Day, I answer a list of questions that I made up. For example, "What is the best thing that happened all year?" "What is the worst thing?" What is something I learned this year?" And of course, a few goals to set for the new year.

A year later I look over the answers. Interesting. And that's all I'm going to say about that. I would, however, recommend jotting a few things down. You don't have to set goals or make resolutions, but just for fun put something on paper, put it in an envelope, seal it and look at it on the first day of 2021. It's a good way to take a personal look at the year that just ended.

We can all agree this was some year for politicians. Shouting, there is so much shouting. And joking. What would late night show hosts talk about if they didn't have the looney political scene to talk about? Political cartoonists must be loving all this.

But some really good things also happened this year. There has been good news of medical research breakthroughs. Multiple scientists finally got a great photo of the Black Hole, something I've always been fascinated by. When I told my friend about the jubilant scientists, she said, "I thought your big ole purse was the black hole."

Anyway, closer to home Douglas Ave. has never looked better with flowers, new buildings, renovated buildings and people walking around spending time in the metro area. The beautifully renovated carousel at Botanica is giving children a thrill.

We rejoiced when babies were born to family members and friends and cried when loved ones passed. It's all part of living through another year.

Some belongings can bring you joy. Swimsuits are not among them
May 15, 2022

Sitting here with 46 other people in a court room, it is silent, actually more silent than church. People are reading the paper, looking at their phones, staring into space or looking at their lap. Jury duty. Will I be picked?

Usually, I would be hoping that I'd be chosen for jury duty because I find it interesting and know it's my civic duty. But this time I'm sitting here writing and hoping I will be dismissed. I need to be home working because we're getting our house ready to put on the market.

My goodness we (mainly I) have accumulated a lot of stuff in the past 36 years. I am sentimental so I have tons of items that bring me joy. Aren't we supposed to keep those things that bring us joy? In one drawer, however, there was no joy. It was full of swimsuits. If you have read my column for years, you know that every spring when swimwear season begins to rear its ugly head, I want to speak sharply to any person who has ever designed a swimsuit

That said, what am I doing with nearly 20 swimsuits stuffed in a drawer? The only one I wore last summer is in my tote bag. And let me tell you it was worn only among close friends in private pools.

Looking at the selection (all one-piece) I nearly laughed out loud. A yellow polka dot strapless? What planet was I on the day I bought that bad boy? And the neon orange one that looked like a pretty coral color in the catalog should have been sent back. At the bottom of the pile was the striped suit that promised to visually eliminate 10 pounds. The only thing it eliminated was money from my checking account.

Seeing this extensive collection my friend asked, "Didn't you try these on at the store?"

The answer is no. It's difficult enough going in a dressing room, sometimes the size of phone booth, and taking off your clothes, then shimmying into an item that will not accent the positive, regardless of what the salesperson said. Not to mention, as I've said many times, it's like putting a marshmallow in a drinking straw. If you're like me, once you get the darned thing on and see flesh that has escaped the "straw," you wonder if your immersion in water should be limited to a private hot tub, the shower or your bathtub.

And dressing room lighting is not flattering, actually the opposite. It seems there's a green cast to everything. Note to stores: Put pink light bulbs in there and watch your sales skyrocket.

You would like to see yourself in a three-way mirror because craning your neck to see over your shoulder doesn't give you a clear picture.

A three-way mirror is helpful to me because I need to check the veins on the back of my legs — the ones that look like a road map to Kentucky. But looking in a mirror that shows all angles usually means stepping out in the common area of the dressing room where someone might see you.

My mom and I would shop for swimsuits at Innes Department store. Many times we laughed so hard we had to sit down. She had no problem going out and looking at herself in the three-way and always insisted I should too. Heck, she went out into the store in a swimsuit to get a different size one time. The saleswoman nearly had a heart attack.

One time I decided to go swimsuit shopping in Topeka thinking that since I was out of town I wouldn't run into anyone I knew.

I went to the dressing room closest to the big three-way mirror. Not being totally disgusted by how the swimsuit looked,

I slipped out to the big mirror.

"Well, hi, Bonnie Bing!" a voice came out of nowhere. "What are you doing here?" she asked. "Just doing a little shopping," I answered jumping back into the dressing room and shutting the door in less than three seconds. I asked her what she was doing and hoped I would recognize her voice. I hadn't taken time to see who spotted me. Turns out it was my neighbor from down the street. The same thing happened in Kansas City, but I didn't know the woman. My new rule is to be at least 500 miles from Wichita if I'm shopping for a swimsuit.

As we age it becomes more and more evident that gravity is not our friend, so I decided to order my swimsuits from catalogs or online. That didn't last long because not once, but twice I thought they sent the wrong suit. It was sad how when I tried them on, neither looked anything like the swimsuit the smooth-skinned, wide-eyed, flat- bellied teenager was modeling in the photo.

So now I have a collection of swimsuits, one with a side cutout that I always try to put my leg through and several that belong on a Hawaiian island. I don't think they'll make the move to the new house.

But here I am, still sitting in a Sedgwick County courtroom writing and waiting on the judge and attorneys. I'm thinking of all the work I have at home.

Next, I'll empty the drawer jam packed with coverups. Not much joy, but it will be more fun and less angst than the swimsuit collection.

When it comes to real friendship, there really is no age limit
February 8, 2015

Who is your oldest friend? No, not the person you've been friends with the longest, the one who has lived the most years. Who is your youngest friend? If both of those friends are close to your age, you have some work to do. At least in my opinion you do because I believe strongly in having friends who are decades younger and also decades older.

We're not talking acquaintances here, but people you would introduce as a friend. I loved the story in *The Eagle* by Deb Gruver about the 94-year-old man who had struck up a friendship with a couple of young women, 21 and 19 years old. It reminded me one of one of my friends, Betty Hedrick, who was a dear friend and at least 30 years older than me. We had lunch together often and shopped and laughed. She tried to teach me to paint with water colors. People who didn't know us would ask if she was my mom. No, I had a great mom so I didn't need another one, but you can always use another friend.

Betty was so much like my other friends – fun, witty, loved fashion, art, movies, beautiful houses, etc. But she did teach me more than she would have imagined. And that is one of the added perks of having friends who have been around longer than you. When I would come through her back door and immediately recline on her couch, she knew it was time for her to shift into therapist mode. She never let me down. It was a huge personal loss when she died, and I still miss her. That's the only downside of having friends older than you. Chances are they will leave this earth before you.

That doesn't stop Ann Sundgren, 52, from being friends with a 94-year-old woman. "She is the mom of my best friend, but I've known her for years, and yes, I consider her a friend." Ann says that Lois has surprised her a few times by being very open-minded and not easily shocked. After seeing a play with Lois that had some R rated language, Ann said something about it. "She repeated some of the language and told us it was nothing she hadn't heard before. We died laughing," Ann said.

When I taught school in the 1970s, a student that was special to me then and is now a friend, Shelly Young, 55, agrees with me on the importance of having friends in a wide age range. Shelly says while the friends she sees most often are in the range of 30 to 50, she also has lots of friends ranging in age from 60 to 90. "I enjoy them because they are the leaders to me. I look to my older friends as the foundation of my life, my inspiration and examples of directions I can go. My older friends are where I get answers to any questions or fears about life that I have. Their experiences help guide my future," she said.

Shelly says she doesn't often see or hear from her friends who are teenagers or in their 20s but feels blessed to have them. "It helps keep me in the loop of what is happening with younger generations and what is important to them. They're my link to the world," she said. But adds that sometimes they are the ones who make her wonder, "What is the world coming to!" Her old teacher had to stifle a laugh at that one.

Angela Cassette, 32, says the main advantage to having a wide age range of friends is perspective. "You get to see the world and situations in a different way, from their perspective," she said, citing the example of an older woman who said she was glad to be in terrible pain because it let her know something was definitely wrong and she needed to seek medical attention. " A younger person probably wouldn't think that way," Angela said.

After chatting with several people my dear friend of 40 years, Cheryl Horton, 62, summed it up: "When you are truly friends, age doesn't really enter into it. A friend is a person with whom you have connected and care about, whether or not that person is a contemporary."

Go make a friend who isn't close to your age. You'll learn a lot from them, and they'll learn from you. If you already have that friend, make sure you nurture that friendship. It's a gift.

Thanksgiving memories drive home sense of family, tradition
November 23, 2014

Here comes Thanksgiving, ready or not. This year is going to be different. I can remember very few Thanksgivings that my mom and I weren't in the kitchen together cooking. That's a lot of turkey and dressing, a lot of years, and a lot of tradition.

My mom passed away Dec. 28. With help, she was able to come to our house for Thanksgiving, but she wasn't able to be in the kitchen. She made sure, however, that I didn't have lumps in the gravy and had plenty of moisture in the dressing.

She laughed as she reminded me of the first time I made gravy. Things went very wrong, and the gravy turned into a sort of pancake. I flipped it into the sink, called mom and she talked me through the gravy making process. That was many decades ago, but she loved that story and retold it every Thanksgiving and sometimes again on Christmas.

It's so easy to charge through life full steam ahead with the holidays coming around so fast you wonder where the past year went. And if you're lucky enough to have family that enjoys celebrating together, your life sort of falls into a rhythm that is full of tradition, comfort and security. When someone is missing from the group, an important someone who truly celebrated the holidays, it changes the dynamics. That familiar rhythm is no longer there.

I'm realizing the many things I've taken for granted year after year are gone, which makes me wonder if I showed enough appreciation for the work Mom did to make every meal so good.

But with Mom's absence I have stopped to think how glad I am some things won't change. For example, how much fun it is to tease Peggy, my sister-in-law, about her "homemade" pies, how funny it is when my brother and husband smart off to each other and both think they're hilarious. Peggy and I sit and have a cup of coffee after everyone else has left the table. It's our little tradition, and I hope we do it for many more years.

If someone complimented Mom on a dish, she would say, "I stirred in a lot of love." With each year she was able to do less and less, and she finally agreed we could switch from her house to our house. At first it didn't feel quite right, but soon we were in the full holiday swing.

Yes, this year will be different, but Mom wouldn't like it if we didn't get together. I wouldn't like it either. Nothing makes me happier than gathering family around our antique dining room table. Mom will be missed, but since she taught us the importance of family, the necessity of sharing, and the taste of love stirred right into the food, we will do fine. We'll make some memories, continue traditions and get back into the comfortable rhythm of the holidays.

And I will never take any of it for granted again.

Aging gracefully means living your best life
November 22, 2015

Several months ago I was asked to give a talk to a group of Junior League of Wichita sustainers. The organization is called Wit & Wisdom. The fact that I'm supposed to be retired didn't deter them a bit. They even suggested a subject: "How to Age Gracefully."

That's a new one. I used to do nearly 60 talks a year and that was for 30 years. But not once did I speak on this subject. It was a challenge, so I decided why not do it. I had a lot of time to figure out what to say. Then all of sudden it was Thursday, and I was trying to decide what to wear to talk to this outstanding group of women.

In the past weeks I've read several articles, but they all said the same old "age is just a number, love yourself, love the skin you're in, do crossword puzzles, exercise, blah blah blah." All good advice. But somewhere along the way I decided perception is what it's all about.

It was time to check in with some perception experts: My Girl Power group at Jefferson Elementary. They are fifth graders, and we have lunch together every Wednesday. I asked them "How old does a person have to be before you consider them old?"

Answers ranged from 30 to 60 years old. Thirty! I asked the girl who had answered 30 why she decided on that number. She said, "Because my mom is 30 and she acts old. She says her back hurts." The girl who said 40 was old said, "My mom is 44 and she's always saying she's old."

Our *own* perception is where we need to start. Thinking that you're an old person will age you faster than you can count the age spots on your hands.

Sixty years old was the most common answer from the seven girls. Then I bravely asked them to guess my age. I made sure I sat there smiling because we all know we look younger when we smile. (I learned that from those articles.) Thank goodness no one said, 80. Guesses ranged from 50 (bless her heart) to 63. When I told them my age, I heard a quiet, "wow, that's kinda old."

I didn't think about my age at all until I hit 65. There's something about all that paperwork you do with health insurance and retirement that drags you into reality. A 50th high school reunion is another not-so-gentle reminder.

But even if we have to scroll *way* down on the list of years to get to the year we were born when filling out something online, it's not time to wind down, it's time to gear up.

Putting it simply, at a mature age we have to look as good as we can, feel as good as we can and do the best we can do for ourselves and others. I have found it's more satisfying looking forward instead of back. Those jeans are never going to fit again, my joints will never again be pain free, wrinkles come, but don't go, and young people will think of me as an older person. Just don't say elderly.

All that is just fine because there are a lot of things in my life that are far more important and a whole lot more fun to think about.

You better take cover: It's swimsuit-shopping time again
April 28, 2013

Ahhh, just when you thought it was safe to come out of hibernation, the stores are filled with tiny garments that are meant to be worn in the water. Yes, swimsuits. We can't call them bathing suits because bathing suits were made of more than four patches of fabric. Bathing suits had boning, and padding and yes, even zippers at one time. You will find none of the above in today's version of swimwear.

That is probably a good thing, but as I looked through a catalog I got in the mail I was stunned to see a black swimsuit that was truly the teeniest I've ever seen. The model was so thin it was a good thing the suit wasn't striped because she would have had just one stripe on the whole thing.

The top was made of two small triangles and a string. The bottom was made of two medium triangles and a string. And if that wasn't a jaw dropper for you, the price of this exquisite little (!) number was $300. Wait, now what? Yes, three hundred smackers. True, there was a tiny little gold clip on the string with the designer's logo on it, but it wasn't 14 karat gold for Pete's sake.

I saw an article in one of the 10 fashion magazines I read that said this is the year to wear a trendy, mis-matched, two-piece swimsuit. No, no it's not. Remember when you were a kid and you could find the top of one suit and the bottom of another, but you didn't care, you just wanted to get to the water? Well, it appears that's the look some are going for. A floral top and a striped bottom. As if this category of fashion isn't tough enough to deal with.

I've had to wear a swimsuit this winter for my water exercise classes. I've nearly worn out my favorite suit so now I'm getting extra activity trying to keep the straps up. I traded off and started wearing another suit, but it's so much like a straight jacket I can barely get it on by myself.

Yes, this means that I will have to travel 500 miles out of town to get a new swimsuit. Remember that's my rule ever since I was in Kansas City looking in a three-way mirror when I heard a perfectly formed woman say, "Aren't you Bonnie Bing?" There was no convincing her I wasn't me.

I can't order another suit from a catalog because when I got one, I looked so different from the model in the photo I thought they had sent me the wrong swimsuit. The last time I tried one of those "instantly slimming Miracle suits," I decided the name came from it being a miracle I could get it over my hips. "Look ten pounds thinner." Right. All I could think about was the old "marshmallow in a drinking straw" concept. I was a living, shallow breathing example of that as I stood looking in the mirror in a tiny dressing room with that beautiful, flattering fluorescent lighting.

Oh well, buck up, Bonnie. I'm resigned to getting a new swimsuit. But rest assured it won't be one of those where it looks like I'm trying to cover a grand piano with a cocktail napkin.

Good days are often regular days filled with simple pleasures
July 26, 2015

Have you ever ended the day with a sigh of contentment and thought what a good day it had been?

Even if nothing really big happened – no lottery win or piece of good news – but it was just a darn good day.

Looking at the beautiful Flint Hills as I was driving home this week, I decided many good days are regular days filled with simple pleasures. Now, before you roll your eyes and wonder what I've been drinking, think about little things that make you smile or sigh, say ahhhhh, or maybe laugh. Here, I'll give you some examples of what I think are some of life's simple pleasures:

That first sip of coffee in the morning

Taking off high heels and digging your toes into plush carpet

Hearing a toddler giggle

Making a baby smile

Giving, or getting an unexpected gift

Knowing that someone is receiving the flowers you sent

That moment right before you drop off to sleep

Receiving a handwritten note in the mail

That moment when conversation stops around the table as people enjoy the meal you prepared

Finding something so funny you can't control your laughter

When you feel the touch of a loved one taking your hand

And women will relate to this one: Taking off your bra at the end of a long day!

A few weeks ago, I started keeping a gratitude diary. Each day I write down three things I'm grateful for. Looking through it I noticed some of the things I've listed are just simple pleasures. Today take note of the things that bring you pleasure in a small way, or in a big way for that matter. With all the stimulation to our senses that technology provides it's easy to forget a lot of pleasure is derived from what's around us and what we experience.

And remember simple pleasures in life don't have to cost anything, except the little time and attention it takes to notice them.

Remembering a kindness done (or said)
October 30, 2016

When something happens three times, especially if it's good, we take note. Or at least we should.

A trio of pleasant happenings came for me recently. A person I know, but rarely see, told me she remembered a time when we were at a luncheon and she didn't like what she got for lunch so I gave her half of my sandwich. I thought it was so nice of her to tell me I had done that. Lord knows I didn't remember it.

Another woman introduced herself to me and thanked me for something that happened many years ago. Her husband had a surprise birthday party. He called me and wondered if I'd do a short video and wish her a happy birthday. I did it and she was telling me what a fun surprise it was.

What a nice husband and how nice of her to take time to thank me for something that took place 25 years ago.

Then last week a man I know, but not well, told me something I said to him that still makes him laugh every time he goes to an assigned seated dinner. Needless to say my comment he remembered was on the smart aleck side, but if he still laughs I'm glad I said it.

By now you're thinking, what is your point here, Bonnie. Well, my point is: take a minute and remind a person of something they did for you. It can be a kind deed you appreciated and still remember. You could also remind them of something they said that you reflect on, or smile, even laugh when you think of it.

Hearing about your nice deed or telling someone about the kindness they did is always a welcome break. And we deserve a break as we try to ride the wave of a political tsunami, face every day struggles, and continue to hope for the best for the next generation.

Let's make it a point to let people know we haven't forgotten their kindness, the joy they shared or the laugh we had with them.

One more thing: Tell them, don't text them.

Living without a sense of direction
October 28, 2012

I wish I had a dollar for every time I've said, "Don't say 'north' or 'south,' say 'left' or 'right.'"

Many people have told me I have no sense of direction. As if I didn't already know that?

My dad always found it comical for some reason. He had a great sense of direction and laughed like crazy when I went out the wrong door at the rest stop on the turnpike and was convinced my family left without me. I was a kid then, but just last week, I was at the same rest stop, went through the drive-through for a little breakfast and headed back to Wichita instead of toward Kansas City.

Another example: The time in high school when my friend Julie and I headed out to go to the Hutchinson State Fair. We were nearly in Eldorado before we decided we were going the wrong direction.

I've been advised to check the position of the sun or look at the horizon to figure it out. Well fine, I do know the sun comes up in the east and goes down in the west, but that doesn't make anything north, for example, crystal clear. When I've asked, "Yeah, but what about when it's night? How does anyone know what direction they're going then?" The usual answer: "The compass in your brain."

Ahhh, there's the answer. I was born without that particular part. It must have gone the way of the math chip. I didn't get that one either.

I'm not alone in this. I have a friend who said her sister got lost on board a jumbo jet. The pilot wasn't lost; she was lost after leaving her seat to go to the rest room.

Those of us who are directionally challenged know that we have to be very careful to use the tried and true, and usually successful method of navigation. Landmarks.

First you check where you're starting from. Sounds silly, but on the return trip this proves to be important because although back tracking should be easy, it isn't. I've driven directly to my destination and managed to get totally lost trying to retrace the route.

It was very embarrassing recently when my friend Kim was following me in her car and I couldn't find the route I needed. I simply hadn't taken note of the landmarks. "Next time you follow me," she said. But there can be problems if your landmark is mobile, such as a truck, and the darn thing gets driven away. Or the beautiful dress in a store window gets changed out. Note: Check the name of the store, not merchandise. Also don't use signs or billboards as a landmark because some wise guy will change it on you.

I was happy to learn this affliction actually has a name: Developmental Topographical Disorientation. Books have been written on the subject, for example, *You Are Here: Why We Can Find Our Way to the Moon but Get Lost in the Mall* by Ellard.

I only get lost in a mall if it's not constructed in a straight line. One friend told me she not only gets lost in the mall, she gets lost in big department stores. Here's a tip: Notice what's just inside the door you're going in, lingerie, cosmetics, whatever, and be sure you know what level you're on when you enter a store.

We hate the dizziness in the head and weird feeling in our stomachs when we're disoriented, don't we? Remember if you seem to get "turned around," especially if your route involves those darned diagonals, rest assured you're not alone. And if all else fails, ask directions. But don't nod as if you understand when someone says a direction. Go ahead and ask, "Is that right or left?" If they scoff, tell them you have DTD.

A Place at the Table nourishes your soul
February 26, 2016

Lately I've read several articles about the importance of family members sitting down to the table for a meal. Many advantages from this ritual are listed and the term "a place at the table" is used time and again.

While most people I talked to about the phrase say it reminds them of meals with their families, it brings to my mind a sense of belonging, of being welcome in any group at any table. And sometimes when there isn't an actual table.

It would appear some presidential candidates must feel they don't have a place at the table these days. But we all feel that sometimes. It's true in some cases we have to earn a place at the table. And getting to the head of the table also can be a struggle.

Going back to the good old days when people did sit down together at a table to eat, they got more than nourishment. Ask any of your friends where they sat at the dinner table and without hesitation they'll tell you. If you're a young person, I hope you'll still have a spot, your spot, where you land for a meal once in a while. And that it's not in front of a television. "I was always in the same place for meals. Not a question. I sat between mom and my brother George," my pal Joyce Gregory said.

My friend Robin Macy smiled just remembering her place at the family table. "I sat across from Mama and between Dad and my sister," she said. "At your place at the table is where you are beloved and included. A place at the table is your greatest honor," Robin said.

The dinner table is your first social platform. I can remember saving a topic, a secret, or a happening to share at the table. I had a chance to sharpen my debate skills because as teenagers my older brother and I agreed on nothing. I realize now the various points of views, announcements, and discussions wouldn't have taken place if we were eating in front of the television.

Studies show that children who eat at least three meals a week sitting at a table with loved ones are less likely to smoke, do drugs, or have an eating disorder. They get better grades and develop better table manners.

But this discussion isn't about table etiquette, although there is plenty to say on that subject, it's about having a place in a group, at home, at work, where you feel a part of something that is good. Something that gives you a sense of belonging, of being important, and offers security.

That said, in your place at the table you have to ask yourself: What do I *bring* to the table?

This was not a day just like any another - thank goodness

September 24, 2023

Remember the song, "Mama Said There Would Be Days Like This"? Well, I had one of those days recently. Nothing serious happened but I should have stayed in bed that day. Actually, under the bed would have been better.

It started off with me hurriedly putting on makeup. Without noticing, I filled in my right eyebrow *way* too high so I went all over town looking like I was inquisitive or perhaps suspicious. No wonder the guy stocking shelves at the grocery store asked if I needed help finding something.

Next stop was the bank drive through. I wasn't totally prepared so I was looking for a pen in my purse which is like finding a toothpick in a black hole. When I went to put the deposit slip and check in the carrier that gets sucked into the bank, I told the teller there wasn't a tube in place. She said with a sigh, "I guess the last person drove away with it. I'll go get another one. It happens." I thought, well how dumb is that. But when she walked away, I noticed I had the darn thing in my lap.

I'm not proud to say I thought very briefly about not telling her and driving away with it, but then I started laughing and told her I was having one of those days. She laughed too. Pulling out of the drive-through lane she saw me run up over the curb. At this point she had to wonder why I'm allowed to drive a car.

Next stop, a shoe sale. I tried but just couldn't pass it up. Trying on shoes that you can take right off the rack is fun. This day, however, I took off one shoe, started looking around and trying on, oh, probably a dozen shoes, then realized I needed to locate *my* shoe. It wasn't where I started out. It was the first time

I'd worn the shoes, and it would be best to still have a pair. I looked on the floor, on the chairs, on the display tables and then went from rack to rack. There it was. Someone had tossed my shoe on top of a rack of size 6s. Certainly not my size.

On the way out of the store those flashy rings that sparkle and shine caught my eye. I tried one on still attached to box. I liked it but didn't want to buy it. Then I realized I couldn't get it off my finger. I pulled and twisted and my finger started to swell a bit. More pulling, more twisting. More swelling. No go.

I went over to two saleswomen who were chatting and said I was embarrassed to tell them, but I couldn't get the ring off of my finger. It didn't help it was still attached to the little box. One woman gave me the, 'boy, you really are stupid' look, but the other one was very nice. She reached under the counter, got hand sanitizer, gave my finger a squirt and that ring came off clean as a whistle. And sanitized.

Time to go home. Pushing my luck I decided to bake a cake. Got the eggs to room temperature, started mixing it up and moved the bowl slightly. Sadly, it went under the automatic hand soap dispenser so of course soap squirted into the cake mix. Luckily it didn't land on the egg whites, so I took a spoon and carefully scooped out the glob of lavender scented soap.

The rest of the day and evening went without any more self-imposed, unfortunate occurrences. Yep, Mama said there would be days like this. She was right. But she also said, "There's always tomorrow."

Disappointment can be painful, but don't let it get you down
September 19, 2021

Don't you just hate to be disappointed? Most people do. Actually, I can't think of anyone who says "Oh, I kind of like to be disappointed." It is interesting, however, the differences in how people handle disappointment.

Personally, I'm not great at it. If I'm disappointed because something I was looking forward to is cancelled, anger is my first reaction. If COVID has shown us anything, it's disappointment. The list is long for nearly everyone and the disappointments ranged from no prom to a loved one not making it home after being in the hospital.

Psychologists say as an emotion disappointment is a form of sadness. Yes, it is indeed the space between what we expected and reality. And it can be painful.

A therapist once told me some people set themselves up for disappointment by determining exactly what they think they have to have to be happy and fulfilled.

An acquaintance I've known for years seems to be an expert on the subject. Her favorite saying is, "I hate my life because I'm always disappointed."

When she went on vacation it was never as she imagined. I laughed when she said, "I know I'm going to be disappointed in the hotel. They never look like the pictures." She hadn't even left home. I wanted to ask her if was going to be disappointed if she wasn't disappointed.

My friend Nancy thinks having expectations that are too high is the problem. She says if you're disappointed, lower your expectations,

A few years ago, one of our granddaughters said she was disappointed in herself because she had set a goal to save a certain amount of money by the time school started and she hadn't reached her goal. I asked her how much she would have saved had she not even tried to reach the goal. She laughed and said, "not much." So even though she was short of her goal, she was still ahead. That brought a smile. And she learned something.

Heck, maybe disappointment is good for us. Granted you could not have convinced me of that in 2020 when we had to cancel a trip to Italy.

Even with a big disappointment, regardless of the reason, you know you're alive with feelings and passion. I'd rather be disappointed than have a bad case of apathy.

Growing up if I whined to my mom about being disappointed about something she would say, "Well, what doesn't kill you makes you stronger." As a teenager that little saying didn't do much for me, but now I understand.

People I talked to agree that as we age, we seem to deal with disappointment better. After the initial foot stomping and pout mouth, we should eventually see disappointment as a good opportunity for learning something.

If nothing else I should learn to just get over it, sister, and move on.

When a person is disappointed in themselves, they certainly should evaluate and learn something. Speaking from experience here.

Also, as you get older your priorities are different, and we don't sweat the small stuff so much. Bad haircut? It will grow out. Cancelled picnic due to weather? We need the rain. It's the old saying, "When life gives you lemons, make lemonade."

We hope for few lemons, but it's important to take a look at how we handle disappointment.

My very insightful high school friend, Julie Strand, who lives in California, said she handles big disappointments by giving herself some time. "I give myself some time to mourn, to be sad. I think I internalize the disappointment and am quiet and don't talk about it for a period of time. I'm giving myself some time to accept that I'm not going to get what I wanted before I'm able to talk about it with someone I trust," she said.

Thinking it over is so much better than getting angry, placing blame or being negative.

So next time I get disappointed I'm going to hold off on pitching a fit, try to pay more attention to how I'm feeling, what I am thinking, and how I will handle it.

Probably the best thing to do is to take my granny's advice: Make the best of it and get on down the road.

New clarity accompanies signs that youth has departed
August 22, 2013

We have it, and if you don't have it yet, you will someday so ha-ha. It's that moment when you know that yes, you are middle aged and youth is a thing of the past. But that epiphany is a piece of cake compared to that rude awakening that you are a senior, and we're not talking school here.

One of my favorite writers, Connie Schultz, who has essays in *Parade* magazine, wrote one about "Life in the Middle Ages." Seems a young man chased her down in an airport thinking she was someone else. After looking her over from head to toe he explained, "You look younger from behind." Nice. Actually, I would love to look younger from behind.

It is those comments, however, that make us realize that youth took off like a speedboat and we're still standing on the beach.

When I was around Connie's age, 55, I was standing in the security line in the Florence, Italy airport. An older man was standing there with his son talking to him in Italian, of course, but he was looking at me. The son turned and said, "My father said he is sure you were beautiful when you were a young woman." Hmmmm. Thanks. I think.

My sweet husband said, "I think she still is." I could have kissed him. Actually, I think I did.

A friend of mine was at a funeral and when she complimented the minister on what a nice service it was, they chatted awhile before he said, "I bet you were gorgeous when you were young." Guys, guys. Think it over.

But it's not all guys. When a young waitress came back to the table with my tab and credit card, she said, "You are Bonnie Bing?" I told her, yes; she cocked her head to one side. I guessed what she was thinking: "You thought I was younger?" I asked. She said, "Yep. A lot younger." I wanted to tell her to enjoy being a wrinkle-free young person because someday the years would catch up with her too.

Not long ago a woman said to me in the grocery store, "Please don't be offended, but has anybody told you that you look like Bonnie Bing?" When I told her I was Bonnie Bing she acted like SHE was offended, said she didn't believe me and walked off. Wait. . . now, what?

Oh well. Let's face it, we're in this together. We can't read the menu without glasses, an inch-long chin hair appears overnight, our colorists are saying, "It's getting more difficult to cover the gray," our upper arms look like our mom's, one great weekend of eating and drinking makes our jeans so tight sitting is a painful experience, the whole social media thing is mind boggling, and the crowns in our mouths cost as much as one for our heads. With rubies.

But for all the joints that ache, the weight that won't go away, the guilt for not exercising more, etc. etc., this time of life is a blast. Finally, it's very clear what's important. We don't want stuff; we want time with loved ones. We don't want the latest, greatest trendy item, we want laughter and peace of mind.

So, stand up straight and walk right up to that kid with a mouth full of braces and tell him you want the senior discount.

Youth sped away, but happiness is the best revenge.

Shopping for swimsuits doesn't get easier with age
July 7, 2019

A woman walking down the mall started laughing when she saw me. I thought my pants must be unzipped or my hair was standing straight up because it was a windy day, or maybe part of my lunch was on my face.

She stopped laughing and said, "I was just thinking about you!" Oh dear. I couldn't think who this woman was. I didn't recognize anything about her. Thankfully she said, "You don't know me, but I read your column, and I know you do not like swimsuits. I'm going to go shopping for one right now."

I asked her if she wanted to go have a cocktail first, and we both laughed. I told her good luck and away she went.

What I didn't tell her was that I had decided to get a new swimsuit. And maybe a color other than black. I've lost some weight and thought maybe it wouldn't be the devastating experience that it has been in the past. Wrong.

It instantly became clear that the problem is not only the body shape, but skin that has been around a long time starts to hang funny. And not haha funny either. Apologies to Sir Issac Newton, but gravity is not our friend. After trying on the three most modest suits in the store I launched into a serious mood swing, had a sweat moustache, was sort of grinding my teeth and repressing the urge to stomp on the last suit I tried on.

But taking a deep breath, I thought, 'who cares if my old faithful black swimsuits are a little loose here and there, I'm getting out of this little fitting room with all these big mirrors and lighting that makes me look jaundiced and going straight home. That cocktail idea sounded really good by now. I was hoping the woman I met in the mall was having a better experience but wouldn't put any money on it. Looking through those racks of bathing suits brought back memories of when I was a fashion writer and did a trend story on swimwear every year. After rounding up pretty, smooth-skinned, flat bellied models the photographer would shoot their photos while pretending to sunbathe or frolic poolside wearing everything from a bikini to a tankini.

The best article I've seen lately on this summertime subject was by Katharine K. Zarrella at *The Wall Street Journal*. The headline was "Bathe in Glory" with the subhead "It's a cliché that swimsuit shopping is depressing – a false one, given the accommodating array of options." She pictured 26 options from A (asymmetrical) to Z, (for zippers.)

The very clever copy with the attention-grabbing full page of swimwear examples had me thinking maybe I should give swimsuit shopping another try. Almost.

The prices also were attention grabbing. A bikini pictured under Q (for quality) was $405 for the top and $335 for the bottoms. Wait. Now what? Yes, even with my marginal math skills, that adds up to $740 if you want to cover all your important parts. Seems quite a bit per square inch of fabric.

Since 75 percent of the female population seem to worry about flapping-in-the-breeze upper arms, there is a long-sleeve swimsuit available from coverswim.com, $220. The one pictured is a blue and white stripe. Why stop there? Perhaps the answer is the unitard I suggested years ago. And yes, that brings back the visual of putting a marshmallow in a drinking straw.

Questions about happiness bring interesting answers
July 13, 2013

Wonder how many times a day we hear the word, "happy." After a brief discussion with a teenager on the subject of happiness I decided to count. Fourteen times in person and seven times on television someone said the word "happy" or "happiness."

Vicky Reiff, a counselor at Affiliated Family Counselors, hears those words, but usually it's the words "unhappy" and "unhappiness." When she does, she asks the client, "When did you start feeling unhappy?" And "When was the last time you remember being happy."

Asking people if they're happy brings some interesting answers. A 42-year-old woman said "I have to be happy. My life is so good it would be embarrassing to be unhappy."

A 50-year-old man answered, "I'm too dumb to be unhappy." That's a funny answer, but some people think a person of average intelligence is happier than the super smarties. Ernest Hemingway was one of those people claiming, "Happiness in intelligent people is the rarest thing I know."

Now wait a minute. The smartest person I know is one happy fella. Vicky agrees with me that happiness in intelligent people is certainly not rare. But she added, "In some cases very intelligent people have a harder childhood because their intellectual level is higher than their developmental level.

Funny, witty people are smart and they're usually very happy folks.

When I asked my 18-year-old granddaughter what she thought the key to happiness is (by texting her, of course) she wrote back, "Money!" Then she quickly texted again, "Just kidding! I think it's being happy with what you have and not being upset about what you don't have."

You can get very scientific about this subject, for example deciding if unhappiness is situational or historical, and whether brain chemistry is the problem, etc., but let's face it, being happy takes some work. And that goes for everyone regardless of where you are on the happiness scale.

The "be careful what you wish fors" and the "if onlys" are out there and sometimes what you thought would make you happy can be a disappointment instead. Think how many unhappy lottery winners there are. Their dream came true and their life turned into a nightmare. And yes, there are some very happy winners as well, but money can't be the only answer.

Author Lisa Earle McLeod says people need two things to be happy -- purpose and pleasure. I couldn't agree more. Meaningful goals are a part of happy people's lives. They are helping others and being kind.

I think it's so important to take pleasure in the moment you're in. We've all known people who dwell on the past, but even if the past was full of happy moments, those aren't the moments that should be concentrated on now. And it's great to look forward to the weekend or whatever, but it's still taking focus away from the pleasures to be experienced today.

When I gave a commencement speech at Wichita State, I ended it by telling the graduates something that a very wise older lady told me years ago, "Let not the tears of yesterday nor the fears of tomorrow spoil the joys of today."

Be happy.

Some people are just a joy to be around
May 15, 2015

Finish this sentence: I want to be one of those people who ...

Can do math in their head.

Can eat as much as they want and not gain weight.

Can speed read.

Can grow wonderful tomatoes.

Can learn to love exercise.

Can wear high heels all day.

Can brighten a person's day just by chatting with them a moment or two.

I think that last one is most important. Right now, think of three people you enjoy running into because when you walk away you are feeling happy.

I caught part of the conversation that Kelly Ripa and Michael Strahan were having on TV a few days ago. They had a mutual acquaintance, and both said that person made them happy any time they were around him. That made me think of those people in my life who do the same for me, and I bet it's true for anybody they are around.

Think of three people who brighten your day. Don't count your family or your close friends. Think of acquaintances. After some pondering (love that word) I decided the quality these people have in common is joyfulness. It's obvious they love being alive and are appreciative of their blessings. They see the good in people and a smile comes so easily to them it's impossible not to smile back.

I'll give you one of my examples. Karen Humphreys. She is a United States Magistrate Judge for the District of Kansas. The first time I met her was in Juvenile Court. No, I wasn't in custody of the state, but my Court Appointed Special Advocate (CASA) kid was. That was when judges rotated in and out of JV court. She was different than any judge I'd seen there before. I was sure she would rotate out before I was back with another CASA case and was sad about that. I didn't expect to see her again.

But when I ran into her in a restaurant downtown a few weeks after our day in court she remembered me, and we chatted for a few minutes. I walked away several notches higher on the happy scale. Walking back to work, I thought, "Wow, how did she do that?"

We all have family members and friends we love to be around for lots of reasons. Maybe they're funny or insightful. Maybe they are caring and helpful. Maybe they're a bubble left of plumb, which makes them fascinating. And yes, sometimes it's because they boost our spirits. And those are the ones you call or make a point to see when you're needing a lift. Don't you love it when you run into an old friend you've always thought a lot of?

Sue Bair was my teacher and mentor at WSU, and is now a friend. She makes me start grinning from 100 yards away.

But it's also those serendipitous moments when you accidentally come across a person you don't know well, but who makes you happy. And it seems you make them happy just by showing up at the same place at the same time.

Maybe the thing to do is study those joyful people who make us feel good and smile. It all starts with a smile.

The Super Bowl is a day for eating, drinking, and cheering
February 2, 2020

It's finally here, Super Bowl Sunday. For those of us who live in Kansas or Missouri we're especially revved up. You've probably noticed there has been more local hoop-la over this Super Bowl than we've seen in 50 years. But hey, what's a half century when we're going to have a big time today. Every age, football fan or not, everyone is pumped. I went to Jefferson Elementary Monday for Girl Power, and students, teachers and staff were decked out in Chiefs attire, or at least wearing red.

I've gone to lots of Super Bowl parties, but until the last few years I didn't care to watch, but enjoyed socializing. The year Janet Jackson had a wardrobe malfunction during the half-time show I didn't see the mishap or more than 30 seconds of the game. Imagine how pleased all the guys were when I totally guessed what the final score would be and won the prize for being the closest. Funny how there was no applause.

But a small wager makes watching more fun, and my increased interest in football has me ready to tackle the job of cheering and eating nachos.

My husband and I bet $5 on the game. I'm looking right now at not one, but two five-dollar bills tacked to my bulletin board. I've won the past two years. But he got to choose which team he wanted this year. Dang it! Of course he picked the Chiefs. So there I'll be rooting for the Chiefs and hoping I'll lose one of the five dollar bills.

Super Bowl Sunday used to mean I'd serve the chili then go shopping. It's surprising, but these days I'd rather watch big men crush into each other than go find a hot bargain that I'd hide in the trunk of my car for a few days.

Being a Chiefs fan and a Packers fan too, I'm trying harder to understand football. My very patient husband knows the rules top to bottom, even the new rules, so he does color commentary which helps.

He has tried to explain it, but I still don't get the part where one team kicks the ball way down the field, then someone from the other team might catch it and go down on one knee, or maybe just watch it go into the end zone or not touch it and look down on the ball as though it's a rare insect.

Don't laugh. I'm sure I'm not the only one of the 110 million people watching who doesn't grasp every strange rule of this my-team-can-beat-up-your-team sport.

When a player is hurt and lies there on the ground, I instantly think of the panic his wife and/or his mother must be feeling. Not to mention what the player must feel like after being mowed down and jumped on. Who dreamed up this sport anyway?

Well, it seems the game of football came about because a rugby player in England was tired of using only his feet so he picked up the ball and ran with it. He probably got thrown to the ground by an opposing team member and the game of football was born. That was in 1863. Yes, that is a simplified version of the history of football.

Imagine how safe their uniforms were. Ha! We've all seen pictures of football players from the old days with a little padding on their shoulders and wearing leather helmets.

Thank goodness the equipment is better today but think about when a player is flipped in the air and lands on his back. Then several 300-pound guys pile on top of him. At that point even the padding they wear now can't be enough.

Think for a moment how much it hurts when you fall down and how sore you are the next day. This is a game where everyone, even the kicker once in a while, hits the ground. Personally, I don't think we should send a guy on the field unless he's a dead ringer for the Michelin Man.

All right, get your game face on. It's time for the Super Bowl! Eat and drink all you want because it's a national holiday. Of sorts. Go Chiefs!

What have you learned lately?
October 29, 2017

This came to me in a flash. I've decided when I greet a friend or acquaintance instead of saying "How are you?" I'm going to ask, "What have you learned lately?"

Let's admit it, most of time we really don't want to know how that person is, at least not in detail. We say it in passing or with the hope it will open a dialogue that doesn't last long and include health problems.

My high school class had a get together recently and I swear the conversation sounded more like we were at a pharmaceutical convention.

But when you say to someone, "What have you learned lately," it can bring on a much more entertaining, thoughtful, and sometimes shorter conversation.

Here are some examples of what I've learned lately.

Leaf blowing is not as easy as it looks.

We live in an old house surrounded by many giant trees. I thought I'd blow off the balcony with my husband's industrial strength leaf blower instead of sweeping. When I turned that thing on leaves went straight up in the air and landed on my head, in my hair, on my sweatshirt and in my mouth. By the time I finished I looked like a monster coming out of a deep dark forest. And I had spent much longer than it would have taken to sweep. Now when I see lawn maintenance people with leaf blowers, I admire their talent.

Memorizing lines is more difficult with every passing year. I'm in *Baby Jane the Musical*, at Roxy's. Tonight is the last night and you're not supposed to know this because I'm the surprise cast member. I had only three pages of lines to learn and it took me *forever* to get it right. Or at least close to it.

It truly is important to have something to look forward to.

No matter what age you are, life is better when there's something mighty good on the horizon. I was reminded of this when I gave a talk recently. A faithful reader, LeRoy, was there and he pretty much made my day. He explained how he didn't like it one bit when I didn't have a column in the Sunday paper. He laughed and said, "Just run some old ones, we won't remember them." I asked him if I put my favorites in a book would he buy one. He said, "No, because then I'd have them all and I wouldn't have anything to look forward to."

It's not only the big things you plan that give you something to look forward to, it can be little things such as big breakfasts on Sunday morning, lunch with a friend, the last chapter of a terrific book or knowing when someone is getting a note you sent in the mail.

Just for fun give it a try. After you say hi, ask someone what they've learned lately. Disclaimer: I'm not saying it's always going to be positive. When I tried it out on one of my best friends she said, "I learned I hate my job." Well, at least she had come to a realization.

Oh, and be ready because you can bet someone will fire back with, "Well, what have *you* learned lately."

Tragedy a chance to stop and smell the storm-ravaged roses

May 29, 2013

Sometimes a person has to give themself a good talking to. I end up doing this frequently and usually out loud. Yes, it is technically talking aloud to oneself, but it is a good thing, not deranged as some might think.

This time it started when, with broom in hand, I forced myself to face the mess and clean up the flowers that were pummeled in the recent storm. I had the prettiest flowers I've had in a long time, especially this early in the season. But Mother Nature got her underwear in a twist so the wind blew and the hail came and that was that.

Then it came to me. "Oh for Pete's sake, think it over." The fact is I lost a thing, which was absolutely nothing, considering the losses people are facing in Moore, Oklahoma. How a few minutes can change so many lives is truly astounding. Students and teachers started the day going about their schoolwork and jobs, no doubt excited about the end of the school year, for some never expecting it was the end of their lives that was near.

I was at White Elementary in south Wichita the day after the Oklahoma tornado. Every Tuesday this school year I've gone there to have lunch with seven fifth grade girls. They quickly became very special little buddies to me. On our last day I looked at those little faces and couldn't imagine them and the rest of the students in their classes being caught in such devastating circumstances.

It's been a year of interesting conversation with this group. We've talked about table manners, fashion choices, the problem of bullying, how to get along with siblings, their highs, their lows, and I've answered lots and lots of questions. Many times, a question would start out, "Miss Bonnie, what do you think about . . . ." and I was usually able to come up with an answer. But when a very insightful girl in the group asked, "Why do bad things like a tornado hitting a school have to happen?" I knew she wasn't asking for a meteorological explanation. I told her I simply didn't know.

But I do know hearing of a tragedy is an opportunity to reflect on how fortunate we are when we aren't personally affected by tragedy. And it's a time to find a way to assist those who need our help.

"It is not a time to get upset and pout about a ruined flower garden," I said to myself as I put the broom away.

That feeling of "Home" is truly one of life's blessings
August 18, 2019

How many times have you walked in your house, dropped your suitcase and muttered, "Ahhh, home." Or maybe you've felt that way when you've arrived at a place you've visited before. It's even possible you've had that "welcome home" feeling when you've arrived somewhere you've never been.

The first time my husband, Dick Honeyman, arrived in the train station in Florence, Italy, he turned to me and said, "This is great. It feels like home." We've been back to Italy several times and now I have that feeling when we arrive.

But as much as I enjoy traveling, I always love getting back to our old house on the river. It's been home to us for more than three decades. There's great comfort in that feeling.

It's not only a person's house that bubbles up this emotion. It has to do with familiarity. That's why it can change over time. The best example is when you physically move from one house to another, especially if you're making other changes in your life.

When I moved on August 1, 1985 I was used to living alone in a much smaller house. The next day Dick moved in and we got married in the living room August 3, the very next day.

Instantly I had a husband, a new home, two teenage kids and one cat. I remember wondering how long it would take before it all felt like home. Now it all is so much "home" it is part of my very soul.

When my friend Teri's house burned and was completely destroyed, she and her husband built another house, much like the 100-year-old house they had had. When she had an open house, I loaned her some things to put on the tables so it looked more like home. She said, "I hope this new house feels like home soon." And a few years later she says it certainly does.

Robin Macy who lives with her husband Kenny White in a charming little house on the grounds of the Bartlett Arboretum in Belle Plaine says she considers the out of doors her home. "I rest in what I call the bunk house but feel more at home out in nature." Makes sense when you remember home is where the heart is.

That "homey" feeling is a result of emotions spurred by not only familiarity but memories. Regardless of how old you are, going back to your childhood home feels like going home. When my mom moved from the house I grew up in, I walked around with my mind flooded with memories. For example, remembering how she allowed my brother to work on his bicycle in the house because it was too cold outside. He did a test ride down the hallway. Dad taught me to parallel park in the street in front of the house. We had one window air conditioner in one room. A new stove for mom that was turquoise blue. So many memories.

But let's be real here. Don't think for a minute everyone gets a warm fuzzy feeling when they remember a home from decades ago.

A friend confided in me that the first home she loved was her dorm room in college. She finally felt safe. She said every time she went home for a visit her stomach would start churning about five miles from her parents' home. I can't imagine.

Recently as I was driving downtown to have lunch with a friend I was thinking about "home" being a good topic for a column. At a stop light I noticed a woman sitting on the steps of St. Paul United Methodist Church. It appeared the big bag next to her with a blanket rolled up on top contained her worldly goods. One minute later I saw on north Topeka a homeless man sleeping on the sidewalk. I would doubt the word "home" would conjure up the same emotions with these two people as it does with people who actually have a permanent home.

It reminded me once again how grateful I am to have a home. To have lived in homes all my life that have been safe and welcoming. And to now have a home where our family and friends feel welcomed and comfortable, where I hear "Ah, I'm so happy to be back," it is music to my ears.

Regardless of the size of the house or how many people live in it, if it's a home you're always happy to return to, you are blessed.

Meeting a goal, any goal, gives a sense of pride
June 19, 2022

When I saw a guy looking in a store window using his reflection like it was a mirror, I thought "Now there's a guy who is proud of his looks." He fixed a lock of hair so it fell just right on his forehead, then sort of strutted down the sidewalk as if it were a New York fashion runway.

Arrogance? Confidence? Self- assured? Pride?

The word "pride" is very tricky. Pride walks a very thin line because it can easily lean toward arrogance, but far on the other side of the line is a lack or complete absence of self-esteem.

I once had an editor who came from a southern state. She told me how she was amazed how Kansans were very reluctant to accept compliments or praise of any kind. She was the second person who came from another state who said we Kansans are "too humble."

Pride can boost self-esteem but also can be so very destructive. How many times have you seen a person disregard an expert's opinion because of pride? How many times have you seen a "proud person" make someone feel less intelligent, less talented, or simply less?

When that has happened to me, I reflect on what my dad told me when I was starting 7th grade. He said there would always be someone who is smarter, prettier, more athletic, someone more popular. "None of that matters. If you do the best you can do, then you can be proud of yourself," he said.

Talking to a friend of mine about his daughter, he said, "She has no direction. She doesn't do much and she has nothing to be proud of."

I told him she needed a purpose. I think purpose and pride go hand in hand. mainly because somewhere in there comes accomplishment.

Accomplishing a goal, regardless of what it is, gives a person a sense of pride. Instead of hiring someone to do a job, do it yourself. Regardless of the job, I guarantee you'll feel a sense of accomplishment and if you're pleased with the outcome, be proud.

Mentoring a young woman at Wichita State University who was the first person in her family to graduate from college, let alone earn a master's degree, was a total pleasure for me. And needless to say, the diplomas were a huge accomplishment for her.

When I told her how proud I was of her not only as a student but as a person, she said, "I am proud of myself." She had always set high standards for herself, and it took her a long time to gain confidence and feel self-assured. She had grown into a fine young woman, but that was the only time in six years I heard her express pride in herself.

Yes, pride can be destructive and in some cases misunderstood, but without some pride in ourselves we don't move forward and continue to make and accomplish our goals.

Perhaps Queen Elizabeth II had it right when she said, "The pride in who we are is not a part of our past, it defines our present and our future."

And considering the problems we have today in this country and in other parts of the world, it's important to remember we still have to start with ourselves. A good start would be to accept ourselves and others and be ready to help when needed. Then we can all be proud.

How to cope with stay-at-home orders? Some try wine, comfort food, and online shopping
April 5, 2020

Well, isn't this something?

Bet you aren't asking, "What?" Yes, I'm talking about the virus that has us under house arrest without the ankle bracelet.

We're getting all kinds of suggestions of what to do while we're at home from every communication method known to man. I'm taking the advice to heart.

For example, we're supposed to do things around the house that we've put off. Let me say here that we would have to be quarantined for a year before that long list would be completed. I have, however, painted bathroom cabinets, cleaned out drawers and cabinets and asked myself 1,000 times, "Where did all this stuff come from?" Guess the spices from 1988 came from the grocery store and the 52 T-shirts came with participation in charity runs, walks, shows, etc. in the past several decades.

And photos! I started going through about 2,000 of them (I'm not kidding) and two hours later nothing was accomplished except a wonderful trip down memory lane.

It also has been fun finding things I thought were gone forever. And several things I didn't even know I owned.

But it's the attic that's killing me. Thirty-three years of dust and an enormous accumulation of Christmas decorations, old toys, old documents, furniture, and who knows what else is a job I've put off for, oh, I'd say about 25 years. When my brain sees a wide, open space it says, "Filler er up, Bon." And I did. My bad.

After 12 hours up there, I haven't made a dent in it. I took today off but I have to go back up those stairs tomorrow or it'll be another 25 years. Hey, maybe that's a good idea, then it would be someone else's problem.

My friend, food writer Adriene Rathbun, says it's the perfect time for comfort food. She's right. I've cooked more in the past few weeks than I did all last year. I made something where I actually followed a recipe, and my husband said it was delicious. He doesn't use that adjective loosely. Maybe I should follow a recipe more often. Comfort food is so good, but it is usually more caloric.

Oh well, like my friend Julie Fitzthum said, "Remember the 'Freshman 15?' Now it's the CoV19."

My, but doesn't wine go well with comfort food. Or most anything. I used to have a rule to drink wine only on the weekend. But listen, these days I don't even know what day of the week it is. I used to be a bit mystified when my mom wouldn't have any idea what day it was. I wish I could tell her I now understand.

I was excited this morning because today was my Book Club. At 11:30 we all struggled to get on the Zoom site that would allow us to talk and see each other. Sort of. It took two tries but I could finally see AND hear everyone. We all talked at once, only half of the group was able to join in, but it was still fun to see the ones who managed it.

One thing I've decided to do is send a note to someone every day. I started with our youngest granddaughter. I found a postcard I bought when we were on our trip, wrote a note and mailed it to her. She was so happy to get it she called. She didn't text; she called! Try it. Send a note to someone who will least expect it. It's fun to get something in the mail besides bills and catalogs. If you get something, call, don't text.

Many of the lists of what to do during this time suggests "learn something new." When I saw a tutorial on how to round brush while drying your hair, I thought, 'Aha! I've never been able to do that.' The woman on YouTube has the same haircut as I do and I had the right brushes from when I tried to use a round brush and blow dryer at the same time several years ago. It seemed I needed three hands to do it, so I gave up.

So I watched the very attractive woman on YouTube and decided to give it another try. She was fast and made it look very easy. And her result was exactly the look I want.

Who knew you could get hair going in two directions wound up in a round brush? Yes, I got my hair on top wrapped in two directions which meant the brush was stuck. The woman on the screen never mentioned this problem. She just kept adding volume here and there and bouffing up her do, talking and looking glamorous the whole time.

Thirty minutes later I had most of my hair unwound from the brush and cut the rest of it off. If you just heard a thud, it was my hairdresser, Melissa Tinker, hitting the floor. Little does she know I'm going to cut my bangs so I can see where I'm going.

Speaking of hair, I have one friend who won't FaceTime because her roots are at the two-inch mark. Like nobody knows she colors her hair?

And yes, like many of you I've done some shopping on-line. So the way I see it now, by the end of April I'll see the results of the wine, the comfort food, and the shopping. And come out of quarantine a nearly broke, overweight wino with a clean attic.

We're in this together. Stay well.

Friends Lisa Corbin and Bonnie Bing

Doing favors for friends can lift your spirit
August 10, 2020

Resilience is what we need in these interesting times.

Now you're thinking, "Well, no kidding, Skippy," but it's so true.

This pandemic is one big challenge that isn't going away as quickly as we had hoped. Resilience is a necessity because heading toward depression and despair is a slippery slope. And it's a place that's difficult to get out of.

I've marveled at many people who have been faced with tragic events and manage to come back from it.

Those are the people, and I'm talking about people of all ages, who manage to get back on an even keel after hitting a bump in the road of life. Or if they fall down on that bump, they get back up and make notes where the bumps were.

A few days ago, I started feeling anxious, or mad or bored, actually all of the above. I've never stayed home so much in my life. For a while, completing projects that had been put off for months, okay, years, was rewarding but the thrill of that satisfaction has given way to a lull. I told my husband that it seems the more I do, the less I get done. At this point the "less" was winning.

I gave myself the old "Snap out of it Bing," pep talk and decided to concentrate on the good. And to do good. A few favors for friends lifted my spirits some. And boosting my attitude of gratitude helped as well. Being positive and concentrating on all the good things in life yanked me out of the dumps and got me going again. Resilience was restored and part of the remedy was to just stop and think and breathe. In his book *Resilient* Dr. Rick Hanson says that breathing can do a whole lot to boost your resilience. He advises taking some big breaths and exhale slowly. That slows the heart rate. He says this will "pull you out of verbal activity, which is a driver of rumination and worry."

He explains that with deep breaths a part of your brain, the insula, is engaged and you reduce activity in the default-mode network, which is the basis for rumination. Who knew there was a default-mode network in our brains?

Anyway, Dr. Hanson says even three deep breaths will make a difference and if you have kind and caring thoughts while taking these breaths, it's even better.

Of course, after reading that part I had to give it a try. A couple of times a day I would stop and breathe and think of loved ones. Sure enough I felt happier, more resilient and determined to get through this pandemic and help others do the same.

Deep breathes might not put you in the mood to clean the garage, or for the millionth time figure out what to have for dinner, but in time maybe you'll notice a boost in your positivity and resilience. Give it a try. It's fewer calories than wine and it's Free.

During this pandemic memories are priceless
August 16, 2020

Here we are, still riding the Coronacoaster. Some days we actually know what day of the week it is. We take a walk, clean out the linen closet, bake something yummy and read a good book. And we think, "This stay at home isn't so bad."

You're up!

The next day it might take heavy moving equipment to get you out of bed. For breakfast you eat whatever the kids didn't finish. One more day of virus-imposed agoraphobia and you're ready for an adult beverage at 10 a.m.

You're down.

Wall Street Journal columnist Walter Russell Mead wrote "Covid-19 is less a transient random disturbance after which the world will return to stability than it is a dress rehearsal for challenges to come." Dress Rehearsal? I'm not questioning Walter, but if this is a dress rehearsal, then let's get this performance over with and head to the cast party. Soon!

I've been told I'm a people person. I must be because I miss people. I miss my pals, my family. Heck, I'm finding I even miss people I don't particularly care for.

If there's one thing I know about this very interesting time in our lives; We-are-all-in-this-together. A pandemic gives us too much time to think about stuff we want. Here's an example. Do not judge me.

For some time, I have wanted a push lawn mower, but not one with a motor, or is it an engine? Anyway, I wasn't t sure why I've wanted it, but I reached the gotta have it point and ordered one. A few days later it arrived on our doorstep.

Imagine my husband's surprise when he brought the box in from the front porch. "Did you order a lawn mower?" he asked with an interesting expression on his face.

"Yes I did," I told him in a very matter of fact tone. Bless his heart, after 35 years nothing seems to surprise him anymore. He did, however, ask, "And you needed this because....?" My quick answer: "Because I wanted it."

But then I came up with a very practical reason explaining I could set the cutting thingy high and mow down stuff that grows above ground cover.

The description of the mower said "easily assembled." They lied. Well maybe it would be an easy task for a mechanic. I've been down the Easy Assembly Road before.

First thing was making sure all the parts were included. They were. Next step was putting two pieces of the handle together. I looked at the picture on the box. Then the instructions, written in no less than four languages, and the sketch of what went where. After carefully studying the step one drawing I put the parts together, tightening the bolts as tightly as I could. It was wrong. I had it on backward.

With much straining and muttering a couple of unladylike words, I got the thing apart, then proceeded to put it on incorrectly again. More muttering.

Third time was a charm. And the next part went more smoothly. Finally, I got that devil assembled!

And at the first push I heard that whirl of the blades.

That was it! No wonder I wanted a push mower. That sound flooded my little brain with memories of my granny pushing the mower across her little front yard in Latham, Kansas and my dad mopping his forehead after mowing the yard on Arkansas Street in Lawrence.

No loud noise from a power mower, but a soft whirring that lets you know you're cutting something. Granted I wouldn't want to cut our big backyard with my new mower, but it's something I'm glad I own. It brings back memories and those are priceless.

When preparing to move, sentimental people are at a disadvantage
July 10, 2022

It seems the buying and selling of houses is continuing at break neck speed. We're part of the trend. But packing to move at our house is not, however, in high gear. As I look at the books, papers, mementos, datebooks, calendars and photos in my tiny office I can't bear the thought of a.) Throwing anything away and b.) Packing all this stuff, then unpacking it later.

It seems I'm a collector of things I didn't even know I collected. For example, fountain pens. I really like fountain pens. They're elegant, nice to write with and it brings back memories of my dad who wrote with fountain pens for years.

The question is what is the number required for things to be a collection? Truth be told I have 25 fountain pens. I write with only two of them. But wouldn't a serious pen collector have hundreds?

My husband says I collect shoes. And yes, I do have some. A lot. No, I'm not telling you the number. I assured him I was getting rid of a bunch of shoes and boots before the move. The problem is some of them are more like souvenirs from trips we've taken. They bring me joy when I look at or wear them. Isn't that the test for keeping something? Does it bring you joy?

It doesn't help that everyone I tell we're moving instantly has a wide-eyed look followed by, "Wow, you will have a lot of stuff to move." True, but as I'm going through all that stuff, I'm very joyful. Moving proves that sentimental people are at a disadvantage. Friends and relatives laugh when they see the number of photos I've saved. I started going through them and two hours later I had discarded two. And that was only because I had no idea who the people were.

When COVID kept everyone at home I thought it would be the perfect time to go through photos and get rid of some or at least categorize them. Nope, that didn't happen.

A large house with lots of storage just invites people to fill up every nook and cranny, doesn't it? And the attic! What a great place for a little costume shop and the wide open spaces for Christmas décor.

Those of us who save things know we're not hoarders. We know for certain that we may need that particular item in the future. That's what making decisions of what to take or not take so darn difficult. It's not easy to have friends help me because most aren't of the "keep it, you may need it later" mindset.

"You have 30 matching vases, you will never need 30 matching vases for heaven's sake," one assisting friend said. Yes, that is true, but I explained sometimes I served on the décor committee of a fundraising event and needed all those vases for centerpieces. So there.

My dear friend, Cheryl Horton, who lives in Arizona recently moved from a very large house to a medium-sized house. From time to time she called me apoplectic, warning me of the trials and tribulations of selling, buying, and, of course, the move. And the lack of closet space. Finally, they're moved in and she lived through it.

Two friends who live here are moving. One has been searching for months to find a new home with theirs already sold. One has leveled the house they bought and is building. Everyone going through these experiences say the same thing: Moving your home is not for the weak. And we're not talking muscles here.

We've lived in our house nearly 36 years. And we love this house built in 1927. Our backyard goes down to the river and the trees are amazing.

I'm relieved we like and are happy for the family who will move in and make happy memories here. That makes leaving easier.

Even though our granddaughters cried when they heard we were moving from the house they have visited all their lives, we have many happy memories to take with us.

And that's far more important than anything of the stuff we're packing to move.

Bonnie with her granddaughters,
Jamie, Becca and Ashley Honeyman

There are still a few things that robots and computers can't do
March 11, 2018

Funny how you remember something that at the time seemed shocking, and now it's beyond normal. Years ago I saw a show on television where a guy had a computer in his home.

First of all, at that time not everyone had a computer at work, let alone at home. The show was about this man who rarely left his house. He ordered anything he needed on his computer. When he said he was "addicted" I laughed thinking that was ridiculous. Now there are facilities for those people who have let everything in their lives slide because they have to be on their computer playing games or shopping or gambling or watching stuff that they don't admit to watching.

Of course the number is small of those people compared to the number of people with computers, and phones. Think cell phones here. Amazing how you can carry your I-can-also-talk-on-this-computer in your hip pocket. (Ladies, don't put it there because it will, at some point, fall in the toilet. I guarantee it.)

Between robots and computers, I'm wondering what this world will be like in 20 years. I heard part of a radio program on KMUW awhile back about how a computer can write a sports story. It gathers the stats and can report who won the game. The data is put together in sentences and there is the story. Using the term "story" loosely. Where is the human element? Where are the human comments? There's more to life than just the facts, ma'am.

It used to be surprising and usually irritating when I called a business and got a computerized voice asking what I wanted, then instructing me to start pushing this button or that button to get the line I needed. And even then, after all those instructions, you didn't get to talk to a human being.

These days, if a human answers the phone at a business, I'm stunned. And pleased. And get ready. You're going to start seeing more and more robots. Granted they are basically computers, but I put them in a category of their own.

The Wall Street Journal ran an article early this month on how the real estate business is using robots. A person in Santa Clara, California called to make an appointment to see an apartment and was told a robot would meet her at the apartment. When she got there, she got a text with the code that would open the door.

Wait, now what? Instead of a live, knowledgeable person R2D2 met her at the door? Yes, that's what happened. There, on the robot's screen was the face of the real estate agent who told the client to follow Rex the Robot for a tour.

Rex showed her around and the woman ended up renting the apartment. You can bet that was no handshake deal.

My friend Cindy, who was in the real estate business long before cell phones and computers, didn't believe me when I started telling her about robots showing dwellings. She says a lot of "hand holding" is necessary when someone is selling or buying a home. "And when I train someone, I always tell them that good news or bad news must be delivered in person, certainly not in a text or e-mail."

When tech lovers argue on behalf of computers and robots and all things that imitate humans, they claim all these technological advances save us an enormous amount of time and money. I'm not so sure. I think instead of saving time everyone is working harder and harder trying to keep up with this world where everything is so darned instantaneous. Let's take a breath. Look directly into the eyes of fellow human beings. Give them a pat on the back, a smile, a hug, and yes, give someone a kiss from time to time. Computers and robots can't do that. So there.

Now that Barbie is 60, it's time for Boomer Barbie
April 28, 2019

When I was having lunch with my friend Joyce recently we somehow started talking about Barbie dolls. We decided the Mattel toy company is truly missing the boat. Yes, Barbie is 60 years old now and they've sold more than a billion dolls, but think it over, Mr. Mattel. The old girl is 60. SIXTY.

This world needs a Boomer Barbie!

Joyce and I came up with exactly what the Boomer Barbie should look like. For starters, go ahead and add a few years to her. Baby Boomers everywhere will have to have one or two of these dolls. Let's get realistic with these grandkids.

First of all, as the dolls are coming off the production line make sure there is a pattern on the skin, much like crepe fabric. On the underneath of the upper arms, make a flexible flap that will wave when you raise Boomer Barbie's arm.

Forget that thick mane we have seen on every doll from Astronaut Barbie to Computer Engineer Barbie. Boomer Barbie's hair is thinning and at least the roots should be gray.

Boomer Barbie will have beautiful eyes, but alas, she needs an extra layer of skin on each lid and very few eyelashes.

Wrinkles need to go on her neck, especially in front. Oh and those perky breasts Paratrooper Barbie is so proud of? Well, gravity has not been a friend to Boomer Barbie so hers point toward her belly that is no longer flat.

A roll around the waist will add realism. Yes, it makes it more difficult for Boomer Barbie to bend but the truth hurts.

The cute, rounded hips on Lifeguard Barbie aren't at all like Boomer Barbie's hips. Gravity again. Hers have slipped and are making their way to the back of her knees. Which reminded Joyce and me, a few varicose veins are a must on the prototype.

Boomer Barbie's knees should look like tiny potatoes and don't forget the bunions on her feet. See, that's what all those darned high heels did to you, Miss Secretary Barbie.

What should Boomer Barbie wear? A mini, sleeveless sundress? Nope. That ship has sailed honey. Boomer Barbie will have on elastic waist Capri pants and a cute top with elbow length sleeves and stylish, but comfortable sandals. She'll wear her fake designer sunglasses on her head and reading glasses on her nose.

And of course she'll have accessories and the little extras that make any Barbie so special. No pool, three-story dream home, or four-car garage because Boomer Barbie has downsized.

Listen up toy designers, this is what should be included in Boomer Barbie's packaging: A jar of wrinkle cream, a pair of Spanx, her AARP card, extra pairs of reading glasses, hearing aids, hair color, a colonoscopy appointment card, her book club book, vitamins, a wine glass and wine bottle, and a black one-piece swimsuit for water aerobics class.

But the best feature of Boomer Barbie should be the big smile on her face. She should have a grin that shows off those expensive crowns and lets people know she is one happy woman.

Bald or extra hairy: What would Baby Boomer Ken doll look like?
November 10, 2019

After I wrote the column about what a Baby Boomer Barbie would look like, several people mentioned I was forgetting about Ken, Barbie's significant other. "After all, Barbie's not the only one who has seen better days," one e-mailer said. Yes, we're talking dolls here. But we're not talking Ken dolls with dad bods, think grandpa bods.

Let's start at the top: The bald spot. I guess some Kens could have long hair fashioned into a comb over style. With less hair on their head, there should be, of course, abundant hair in the nostrils and ears.

Hair on the back of the head should be very flat from leaning back in his recliner.

A big, comfy sweatshirt would be a staple in this Ken's wardrobe along with his "at home" jeans that end up being worn to the store, to run errands and unfortunately sometimes to the movies.

Running shoes, even though Ken usually isn't a runner at this age, are a must and he's proud that his favorite pair is going on ten years. These are the shoes that should go to wherever all those lost socks are holed up. Speaking of socks, Boomer Ken would always wear his socks, even with his sandals.

A sport coat that won't begin to button around Ken's tummy is an item for his closet because since retirement he hardly ever wears it.

Also in the wardrobe: The very popular T-shirts in a wide assortment of colors. These are the shirts that give fabric a real stretch test. Not so much around the biceps, more around the belly.

The professor Boomer Ken doll would have reading glasses either on top of his head or more likely on a cord around his neck. His casual look is Bermuda shorts, an above-mentioned T-shirt and sandals with black socks.

That ensemble would also be sold with Grandpa Ken, Crazy Uncle Ken, Retired Accountant Ken and the Old Guy Next Door Ken.

And just like his sweetie pie Baby Boomer Barbie, Ken will come with a variety of accessories: Eyeglasses with frames from 20 years ago, a beat up briefcase, a well-worn belt with dents where the buckle used to fasten, a pill box divided into days of the week, a little six-pack of beer, teeny tiny batteries for his hearing aid, an appointment card for his next colonoscopy, his cell phone that he still hasn't figured out, a checkbook and a wallet filled with actual cash, pictures of his grandkids and one credit card. Ken and Barbie, the younger versions, are beautiful, and handsome.

I should mention, however, when I got my first Ken doll many decades ago, my older brother pointed out that Ken was missing a very important part. That's all I'm going to say about that.

Boomer Ken would have wrinkles and yes, maybe more than one chin is called for. But there would be a sparkle in his eye and great big smile on his face. He might not be at his "fightin' weight" but he gets to do what he wants most days and has plenty of time to spend with Baby Boomer Barbie in their big, pink plastic mansion. No downsizing for this duo.

What more could a couple of Boomers ask for?

The Beatles, Fabian, how 50 years ago can seem like yesterday
February 23, 2014

Remember when you marveled at how your grandparents and parents could recall in detail things that happened many, many decades ago? Granny told me exactly how she met Grandpa more than 60 years earlier.

I was amazed, then boom! There were the Beatles on a recent television special them performing on The Ed Sullivan FIFTY years ago? No way. Yes, it is true. It's been a half century and I remember it well.

Everyone at school thought the Beatles coming to America was the coolest thing to ever happen to our country and the show would be by far the best thing ever shown on television.

The magic of television brought the Beatles into our living rooms! While the skinny guys from England with the long, floppy hair sang, I glanced at my mom who seemed amused. Dad simply looked puzzled. "If they're so popular, can't they afford a haircut?" That comment was met with a collective, "Shhhhhh!"

For the next several days Dad would spontaneously sing "Woooo" and shake his head imitating the Fab Four. Of course his hair didn't move one bit because it was slicked down with Brylcreem.

His opinion changed, however, when we were driving to church and "Do You Want to Know a Secret" came on the radio. He let me know that he thought that was a good song and THOSE guys could sing. I was so delighted to tell him it was the Beatles. All he said was, "Well, they still need haircuts." I shook my head and sang, "Woooo."

Speaking of heart throbs – Remember Fabian? Many of you won't because you're too young. Darn you. Anyway, he had a birthday on February 6 and the man is 71 years old! By the way I don't think that's old because in my opinion 70 is the new 40. The older I get the older the "new 40" is.

I guess his age came as a shock because we have watched other performers, Paul McCartney and Ringo, for example, continue to perform as they've aged.

Just like the people you haven't seen since high school, the ones that make your jaw drop at the 40th reunion. Those you've seen from time to time don't seem to have changed that much.

Unlike classmates, when the very handsome teen heart throb Fabian left the public spotlight, I guess I assumed he flew off with Peter Pan and never grew up. Googling him proved me wrong. Just like the rest of us, he's aged.

But here's something I bet you didn't know. According to Wikipedia (all right, not the most reliable source), Fabian was drafted, but rejected, for military service during the Vietnam War. According to USMC Lt. Col. Arthur Eppley, Fabian was declared 4F (unfit for service) after presenting a doctor's note stating that induction into the Army could cause him to develop homosexual tendencies. Wait. Now what?

By the way – If you can't relate to this column at all, save it for a few decades and read it again. Then it will make sense, just like Granny's stories.

How to be a better listener and a better friend
January 27, 2019

Adults are saying kids aren't going to be able to talk to each other because they are constantly texting instead of talking. By the way it appears many adults are falling into that same dark, non-verbal hole.

While thinking about this, it dawned on me people who don't talk may also lose their ability to listen. To really hear someone when they are talking, you have to give them your attention.

It drives me crazy when people on TV interrupt each other. Are they afraid they won't get their allotted time on camera? As a viewer it makes what any one of them is saying impossible to hear. Everybody loses.

On the political scene (holy moly) people don't want to hear an opposing point of view so they interrupt and talk louder than the other person. People, people, volume is not the answer to this problem.

After chatting with a friend about all this I came across an article in *The Wall Street Journal* by Masada Siegel. She agrees with me, asking, "Is listening a lost art?"

She talked to a hostage negotiator for the story. Whoa, talk about someone who would have to know how to listen.

Our conversations aren't usually a matter of life or death, but it is necessary to give a person time to tell their story, to vent, to ask questions or answer questions. If we listen carefully, we're not thinking of what we're going to say next.

I overheard two women in the check-out line at Walgreen's talking. No I wasn't eavesdropping, I was practicing my listening skills. The woman behind me said that her mother had passed away recently and she was having a difficult time getting on with her life. She lives alone and her mom had been her best friend.

She was still talking when the other woman launched into details about her own mother's death 10 years ago. She said, "After such a long illness it was a relief for us when she died. You'll get used to it."

Wait, now what? She wasn't listening or observing the amount of heartbreak the woman in front of her was suffering. She was interested only in telling her own story.

The grieving woman just wanted to talk, maybe even get a little assurance that it will be better someday. Something other than, "You'll get used to it."

My friend, Angie, decided when she went to one of her high school reunions she would be a listener, not a talker. She said she had a blast. She didn't say anything about herself unless she was asked.

But she asked all about what others were doing, about their families and she really listened to their answers. Bet she was one of the few in the room doing that.

Even though I don't text constantly, in this New Year I'm going try to be a better listener. I have no doubt it will result in learning more about and have a better understanding of those who are doing the talking.

Get the skinny on men's leggings
February 23, 2013

We first started hearing about "Meggings" late last year. Yes, leggings for men. Seems some well-known designers thought Robin Hood was on the right track and since skinny jeans weren't nearly skinny enough, they narrowed the silhouette until they were officially leggings.

We're in Kansas and while I had seen a few men wearing them the last time I was in New York, I decided I wouldn't write about this trend until I saw a guy wearing Meggings right here in River City.

It happened. There he was, a tall, very thin man wearing a brown sweater and camouflage leggings. If he thought no one could see him in camo, he was wrong. Sadly.

But more distressing was his sweater needed to be longer. His very narrow, camo covered rear end was exposed which means of course from the front he looked like a male ballet dancer gone bad.

He was at the mall and I wasn't the only one taking notice. One portly fellow said loudly, "Did that guy forget his pants?"

Those ARE his pants, which raises the question: What do you wear under them? As in underwear. Jockey shorts would get all bunched up and tidy whities would give a guy terribly visible panty lines. I have no idea if they make thong underwear for men. I don't want to know and I'm sorry if you're eating breakfast while reading this.

I've read several articles and fashion blogs about Meggings and was surprised to see some of the designers who decided to put them in their fall collections. Givenchy for example. And they're a hot item in London. Just think how happy Boy George is about that.

Justin Bieber has worn them, so has Russell Brand.

All right guys, if you're considering getting some Meggings, take a good, honest look in the mirror. If you've got a big tummy or skinny legs with knobby knees, this is not a look for you. And guys, even though you usually don't have to worry how big your derriere is, in Meggings you have to take note. Just because the Lycra keeps the junk in your trunk from shaking, doesn't mean it's looking good. And you never know when you'll have to bend over. I saw a woman in Dillon's wearing a pair of bright orange tights. She bent over to get a box of cereal from the bottom shelf and I thought the moon was coming up over the Wheaties.

Are Meggings better than seeing guys wearing pants so baggy and so low they could drop at any moment? SURELY the super tight Meggings won't catch on the way the hip hop pants did.

I don't think so, know why? Pockets. Meggings don't have pockets. Where does a guy put his phone? His car keys? His billfold?

Oh, of course. In his man purse.

Rituals are a comfort in life
August 20, 2015

A counselor once told me that rituals are important, not only with your spouse, but with family members and friends. The older I get the more I agree with him. Traditions are important too, but rituals are something different.

Growing up my mom and dad would get up early and drink coffee in the living room. If I woke up early enough I would eavesdrop, but usually it was stuff that didn't interest me. After two cups dad would jump up and go get in the shower and mom would start fixing his breakfast. After my dad died, I think that little ritual was one of the things Mom missed the most.

Sharing a meal is a ritual that in my opinion is very important. It's a time to pause and enjoy not only the company, but all of our senses. My husband and I recently went on vacation to Colorado with our family. Getting three granddaughters at the table at the same time can be a challenge, but it's worth the planning. And when a somewhat wild white water raft trip turned out to be one of the highlights of the trip, Becca, 14, decided it should be a tradition. I agreed but added we should have a ritual of standing in a circle and saying a little prayer while still on dry land.

Maybe doing something the same way day after day gives us a sense of security. Everything and everyone seems to move quickly these days. Call me crazy (many already have), but I get comfort in reading the Sunday paper sitting in the same chair every week. I watch Good Morning America every weekday and miss it something fierce when we're out of the country.

Reading the news, whether the printed version or online, is a ritual many people tell me is important to them. That's why if the paper isn't available, it's a serious problem. It throws you off when something familiar, something you enjoy, is simply not there.

I asked a friend if she had any rituals. She said she didn't have any because she lives alone and every day is different for her. I bet her five dollars she had at least three rituals. I had her tell me about her morning. She had a very definite morning ritual, two cups of coffee, one bowl of Cheerios and she sat in the same chair at the kitchen table and read the paper while she ate. Ritual.

She called her mom at 9 a.m. every morning. Ritual. And she had a definite routine when she got home from work. She got the mail, sat in the same chair to look through it, changed her clothes, poured a glass of wine and read her personal e-mails. Ritual.

After collecting my five bucks, she laughed and said, "Maybe that's why I don't like to go out of town. It messes up my *rituals*."

Another friend says walking her dog, Remy, pretty much at the same time every day is important to her for relaxation and exercise, but knows it's more important for Remy. When her dog Cody died she said it was a ritual she missed terribly and was anxious to get another dog.

When life changes, rituals change. The thing to do is create new rituals, some just for yourself and some with others. It's a comfort, so comfortable, in fact, you may not even notice it, but it's there. And it's all yours.

I'm not ashamed to admit that I loathe summer
July 18, 2021

Summer is my least favorite season. There, I said it. I don't like summer. And every year I like it less.

My friend Cheryl, who lives in Carefree, AZ, agrees with me. You say, "Well of course she hates summer because where she lives its unbelievably hot." But it's a dry heat. Ha! Listen, Bucko, a temp of 119 degrees is hot regardless of how dry it is.

As a kid I loved summer, just lying by the side of a swimming pool on warm cement that smelled like chlorine, fingertips shriveled up from being in the water so long. That was a long time ago when my pals and I didn't worry what we looked like in a swimming suit.

Well, that ship has sailed along with my fondness for summer months. The flowers that looked so pretty in the spring appear to be thirsty most of the time. Sometimes the weather is so humid the air feels squishy. Getting in a hot car after it is in the sun gives you a hot seat and brings on a temper surge. No wonder road rage increases in hot weather.

When I had a conversation with two avid fishermen, I had a revelation. No, I'm not going to start fishing, but we talked about ice fishing. Think how surprised they were to find I was the only one who had actually gone ice fishing. Just remembering how cold it was sitting out on the ice that day made the 95 degrees outside more bearable. Sort of.

When you're really cold it helps to think of a warm fire, right? Try this: As you're crossing the hot pavement in a parking lot to get in your 100-degree car think of jumping into cold lake water or being out in a blizzard or ice fishing.

The only reason I went to a frozen lake to ice fish was that the late Steve Harper, a photographer and the outdoor writer at *The Wichita Eagle,* told my editor it would be great for me to experience ice fishing and then write about it.

How tough could it be? I thought we'd be in a little tiny shack with a heater, comfy camp chair, some hot coffee and tasty sandwiches. Nope, none of the above.

Steve drilled a hole in the ice, dropped a line in the hole and handed me the fishing rod. I said, "So I just stand here until some fish wants lunch?" He said, "No, you sit here," as he turned over a bucket.

I had on so many clothes under my dad's flannel-lined coveralls I looked like the Michelin Man. I was determined to not complain. My feet got cold first. When my nose turned red Steve told me to "think warm." It worked about as well as the above-mentioned method of thinking cool.

Some people say they like winter better than summer because it's easier to warm up than to cool off.

Maybe it depends on a person's body thermostat. Some people say they're hot all the time, some are always cold.

Regardless, I'll bet the die-hard fans of summer are in the "always cold" category and probably still look good in a swimsuit. The rest of us can rejoice that fall will be here before we know it.

Does buying a swimsuit fill you with dread? Try these tips
May 16, 2021

Oh yes, even though the weather is still cool, it's that time of year that smooth-skinned, flat-bellied people look forward to shimmying into a sleek bathing suit and heading poolside.

The rest of us. Well, not so much. Not even a little. Actually, it falls into the category of dread. This year I decided to try for a positive attitude adjustment. If you've read this column for the past 30 years you know that was no small goal.

I thought perhaps if I got a swimsuit that was somewhat flattering, I'd quit hating the people who designed and manufactured them. I'm here to report that so far keeping that attitude is becoming more and more difficult.

The catalogs are arriving in the mail. For starters, could someone in marketing come up with a better headline than "In the Swim" because it's been used to death.

Sad to say I do need a new swimsuit because the two I bought last year look worse than I remember. I thought they'd stretch out like suits used to do, but nooooo. Thanks to all kinds of miracle stretch fibers they maintain their shape. Shouldn't they be like memory form and maintain *our* shapes?

Knowing that some of you out there in Reader Land feel the way I do I've come up with a few tips for those of us who would love if a swim unitard with skirt would be the hot new look. After years of research, here's what I found:

1. Even though you may need an adult beverage afterward, DO try on the swimsuit. Chances are it won't

look like it did on the mannequin or in a photo. I ordered from a catalog one time and thought they sent me the wrong one. Nope, they didn't.

2. Personally, I have a rule. I won't try on a swimsuit unless I'm several hundred miles from home. The second you do shop here and step out to look in the three-way mirror, you hear your name and "Is that you?" It's a take-me-now-Jesus moment that you don't want to experience.

3. Make sure you understand how the suit goes on before you attempt to put it on. If it has some extra straps or cut-outs beware! I learned this the hard way.

A salesperson in a small hotel gift shop in California talked me into trying on a swimsuit. She put me behind a little curtain. I got tangled up in the thing because I put my leg through the cut out that was supposed to expose my side. Then I got the wrong part around my neck. I got tickled trying to get out of it and snorted, (I do that when I'm trying not to laugh). The saleslady thought I was having some kind of medical issue.

4. If you take anyone shopping with you, make it an honest friend. I don't recommend your significant other because that's the person who probably told you, "No, those jeans don't make you look fat." Take an HONEST friend.

5. Try for that positive attitude I'm working on. But I do still wonder: Did all male swimsuit designers hate their mothers and sisters? Do all female designers have perfectly formed bodies, or at least do their models, who had a lettuce leaf and a hummingbird wing for lunch?

6. And last but, certainly not least, be brave! Go in that dressing room with lights that make you look slightly green, or sometimes gray. By the time you get the first

suit on you'll have a sweat moustache and wonder why you're doing this. Stand up straight. You've got this! But no, you cannot wear Spanx under your swimsuit.

There you go, now you're ready to shop. And ponder this: Maybe the problem is looking in the mirror. Once you're tucked into that suit (some of you will understand why I used the word "tucked"), decide if it's comfortable. Can you move around in the water and have a good time? If yes, then get that one. You don't have to look in the mirror if you don't want to.

When you head to the pool, if someone doesn't like how you look in it, it's their problem.

Sweet memories bring comfort
June 23, 2019

One of my favorite sayings is "Let's make a memory."
As I listened to a lecture on Alzheimer's and dementia at WSU's Positive Aging Day, I started thinking how important memories are. Not only are memories your life story, they can lift your heart and bring a smile to your face, even at a sad time.

That happened to me recently when I left a friend's home knowing I would never see her again. My friend of nearly 40 years, Fran Kentling, died a few hours after I left.

Once I started home I thought about the time Fran and I talked some fellow employees in the newsroom into taking part in the River Festival Tug of War competition.

Now, you understand that A, this was not a group of people who took part in many social activities, B, very few, if any, frequented a gym, and C, they were already dubious of the newbie (me) because it seemed to them I stepped out of the elevator from nowhere.

That said we got a team together. I picked up Fran the morning of the big competition. We just knew we'd pull together as a news team and maybe not win, but take second place. Just to be sure we'd be ready we had a mimosa, knowing vitamin C would be good for us.

There weren't enough mimosas in all of Wichita for us to win the contest. We had men and women on our team, all reporters and editors. The first team we faced was made of muscular, flat bellied guys who made short work of pulling us across the line. Fifteen seconds, tops.

I remember one reporter said to us, "I'm sure glad I got up early on a Saturday morning so I could get sand all over me and be humiliated."

Fran and I explained working as a team was good for office morale. He wasn't buying it. It was fun, darn it. Whether they knew it or not.

Because I was totally unfamiliar with the way a newspaper operated when I started in 1980, Fran took me under her wing. If it hadn't been for her, Jon Roe and Diane Lewis and I wouldn't have lasted two weeks. Now all three of them are gone.

Thank goodness for the memories of going to lunch, birthday parties, retirement celebrations, good conversation over coffee and sometimes wine, and stories of their early days at *The Eagle.*

In the last couple of years I've lost several friends and recently several of my friends have dealt with tragedies. It seems there are times the wheels start falling off this thing we call life. If not personally, for those we care about. That's when we have to move forward but find comfort in remembering the good times.

While thinking about the importance of memories I realized there are many moments I didn't value at the time but are now sweet memories.

A friend's life might end, but the memories of the good times you shared don't have to. All we can do is grieve our losses, help each other through tough times and treasure the memories we have.

No one can take them from you.

Sometimes, it's best to say – and mean – that you're sorry
September 8, 2013

Let's get one thing straight, there was no eavesdropping going on. When you're on one side of a huge dress rack in a department store and people on the other side aren't getting along, well, you can't help but hear the conversation.

It went like this: "All right, I'm sorry. There, can we forget it now?" the male voice said. "Oh sure, like you really mean it. You're not sorry, you're never sorry," replied the female. I had to agree that he didn't sound sincere and all he was sorry for was marrying someone who was sensitive.

This little scene got me thinking how very few people know how to apologize. I'm afraid I'm one of those people but I've improved because my husband has made very clear the flaws in what I used to think was a good enough apology.

It's one thing to say, "I'm sorry," it's another to choke out those three little words: "I was wrong." And you don't even have to be totally wrong to say them, but if you are the least bit to blame it's important to take personal responsibility for the problem.

While this might seem like the wimpy position, it's actually not according to business strategist and author Lisa Erle McLeod. "Stepping up to fix your part makes you more powerful, not less," she wrote. She explains being able to say, "I'm sorry, I was wrong," pulls you out of the victim mode and into the action mode. When you don't say it you are powerless because you can't change anything and you can end up trapped in the conflict for a long time, or forever. She also points out with those three little words you get control of the conversation.

We all know people who wouldn't apologize and admit they were wrong if their lives depended on it. And we've all been around people who say "I'm sorry" so many times it's almost like a habit they seem to have developed.

This brings up the matter of who we believe when we get an apology. If it's someone close to us we know their personality and know whether it's a heart-felt, sincere apology, or words said to avoid a scene in public, tears, the silent treatment, a punch in the nose, etc.

The woman I overheard in the store heard the sing-song "I'm sorry" from her significant other one too many times. He sounded like my youngest granddaughter when she was instructed to apologize to one of her sisters, "Saaarreee."

The last time I made a major apology I decided to stand up straight, no groveling, good attitude, I looked the person in the eye and said, "I'm sorry, I was wrong, I was out of line." Of course, by the time I got to the word "line" I choked up, but the apology was accepted and the whole thing was over.

A lot of people will probably disagree with me on this, but the older I get the more I realize you have to choose your battles. Some things simply aren't worth the time, energy and hurt feelings it would take to end up in a conflict.

If he thinks he's right about something, my friend's husband says, "I'll gladly argue until the sun comes up and I will never apologize." My friend said, "I just go to bed and let him argue by himself. He knows if he ever wants another home cooked meal he WILL apologize in the morning."

Well, I guess that's another approach.

DIY, even when it goes south, can create a sense of accomplishment
June 9, 2019

Oprah Winfrey, perhaps you've heard of her, wrote a book about things she knows for sure.

Well, don't we all know some stuff for sure? For example, I know if you decide to do a home project, the DIY concept can go south.

A friend of mine's favorite saying is "Hire it done." That's fine, but sometimes I just know I can tackle a project, finish it and have that wonderful feeling of accomplishment.

The problem comes when you realize just how many bumps in the road there can be. Even if it's as simple as repairing and painting the deck. I thought this project would take about three days.

We have a balcony that wraps around the back of our house, and it was in need of attention. First, I got out my battery powered, super-duper new drill and screwdriver. Getting those loose boards tightened down shouldn't be a big deal. Well, it was, I didn't know there was metal under some of the boards. Just as I was making progress, I dropped the drill bit in the crack between the boards. I decided then all the boards looked pretty good.

Next came getting it as clean as possible, so I swept it off, blew it off and power washed it. Ready to put the new paint on. Went to the big store that carries everything from potato chips to kitchen sinks as well as paint for anything you can think of except maybe live animals.

Decided on a color, Forest Brown, in moderate to heavy texture. Had to wait for the wood to be dry. Got out there, started painting and thought, "Hmmm, that looks kind of orange. The color chart didn't look that orange. Maybe it just needs to dry." I was smart enough to quit painting and it did change color. It became more orange. Not rust, but pumpkin orange.

Back I went to that giant store where the entrance is a city block from the exit. This time I thought Autumn Brown would be perfect. I moved everything to one side of the balcony and painted. Ahh, much better color. Once it dried, I moved everything to the painted side and painted again. I was very pleased until there were three feet left to paint and I totally scraped the bottom of the bucket, out of paint.

By this time, it was the day before leaving for Scotland, so I had to put the thing on hold until we returned. It rained the whole time we were gone so I had to wait several days after we got home to let it dry out. It continued to rain.

In the meantime, I went back to get the paint to cover the three feet. A quart ought to do it. No, it only comes in gallons or three gallons. I bought the gallon, brought it home, started painting and thought, "Hmmmm. that looks a little dark. Well of course it was darker. It was Oxford Brown not Autumn Brown. Sadly, my husband Dick liked the darker brown better and so did I.

Back to the big store where the people in the paint department probably thought I was painting a large house in multiple shades of brown. I got another gallon of Oxford Brown. At this point I wondered if I should just get the three-gallon bucket for a hundred and some dollars just to be on the safe side.

No doubt Dick thought maybe it was time to bring in a professional but to his credit he didn't say so. By this time, I was a determined, nearly frothing at the mouth do-it-yourselfer.

Finally got it painted. Time to get those pots planted! Went and bought plants and of course that's a whole story in itself. At one place I bought so many I had to hold one in my lap driving home.

Ta-dah. It's finished.

Yes, it took longer than three days. I looked it up, this little project was started on April 23rd, finished, including the plants, June 4. I doubt Martha Stewart ever had such an experience. She would have built and decorated a house in that amount of time. We can't all be Martha Stewart.

But wait. There it is, that wonderful feeling of accomplishment!

Forget laugh lines, now there's "tech neck"
July 6, 2014

As if we didn't have enough effects of gravity to worry about, now there's "tech neck." No, it's not that your neck is stiff from clamping you cell phone between your shoulder and your ear, it's a wrinkle. Yes, a wrinkle caused from constantly looking down at your phone, IPad or another device.

We can't frown or furrow our brow without getting wrinkles. Now we shouldn't look down. I think the answer is to do everything in a prone position. Someone told me if you lie on your back and look in a mirror, you'll see what you'd look like with a face lift. If that's true, forget it. Yes, I did the mirror test, and now you will too.

When you take a photo of yourself, a "selfie," (I really don't like that word), or with two or more people, an "ussie" (I like that one even less), remember to stretch that arm out as far as it will go and hold the phone or camera up so you have to look up. Just don't tilt your head back too far or you'll have a photo of your nostrils.

The other day I accidentally hit the camera booth icon on my mac book, and oh good grief. I thought my laptop had been invaded by an alien. But no, there I was with about 16 chins. I still haven't recovered.

Questionable results – If you love reading results of studies, here's one for you. A recent study of 26 countries found that men in Slovenia spend 111 minutes on housework every day. I don't know anything about Slovenia, so I take the researchers at their word. The same study, however, says that men in the United States devote 82 minutes *a day* on household tasks. Wait, now what? That is more than an hour a day. What did they do, ask a bunch of house husbands? If you're one of those 82 minute guys, forgive me, but ladies, isn't that number a little high? Oh, like 60 minutes too high? Just asking.

Your trash is your responsibility. Don't litter
September 13, 2020

Raise your hand if you're a litterbug. Now make a fist with that hand and drop it on the top of your head. People who litter deserve a thump on the head.

At first I thought it was my imagination but then a friend of mine mentioned it. There is more litter in the streets and parks and parking lots than we've seen in a while.

Even if there's not actually an increase, it still needs to stop. We live on a busy street so our driveway, especially on weekends, is a dumping ground for not only beer bottles and cans, but fast-food sacks. Do we throw stuff in your yard and on your drive? No.

I was following a car with two teenagers in it. The passenger opened her door and emptied liquid out of a cup. I was happy to see she didn't just drop the cup in the street. But then she unwrapped a candy bar and threw the wrapper out the window. Grrrrrrr. Liquid is one thing. Paper is another.

Our backyard goes down to the river. Well, yes, you can imagine what goes floating by besides the kayaks, canoes, shells, and paddle boards. Those aren't the people throwing stuff overboard. They respect the river. Others don't. Three weeks ago, I saw lumpy, foamy stuff in the river. Someone downstream decided to dump whatever it was in the river and it floated close to the bank and stopped in some limbs. People! People! The big and little Arkansas are not waste dumps. That includes grass clippings which make the river look like it's covered in moss.

My near obsession regarding litterbugs started in ninth grade when my boyfriend threw a gum wrapper out the car window. His mother shamed him and her words stuck with me.

At the grocery store recently I stepped out of my car into a big pile of cigarette butts and ashes, a few gum wrappers and a wad of gum. The person who parked there before me deserves a flat tire. Even better, four of them.

Our granddaughters have heard me talk harshly (they probably consider it preaching) about people who think others should clean up after them. I'm sure these girls don't litter, but when Ashley was in college I got in her car and I realize I should have extended the sermon a bit further.

"I know it's a mess," she said, "But I didn't litter." I think she used the description of her car having "self-contained litter." That was right before I unearthed a three-week old hamburger.

Yes, there are bigger problems than littering in today's world, very big. But let's not forget the smaller ones. Starting with: Your Trash, Your Responsibility.

From newsroom to living room, hard to write uninterrupted
June 23, 2013

Now where was I? I thought when I left *The Wichita Eagle* newsroom, I wouldn't be saying those words as I wrote a column. But I said exactly that just two minutes ago. And an hour before that.

In a newsroom phones ring constantly which means the room is filled with reporters talking on the phone as they type, talking to each other, humming, whistling, walking by, making coffee, drinking coffee, dropping mail and press releases on your desk, etc. You would think in this quiet house where I now work, I could whip out a column uninterrupted. Tell that to the UPS man – the nine – count them nine, telemarketers, ambulances going by, dogs barking at everything from a squirrel to a leaf falling from a tree, car radios that vibrate the windows, and the list goes on.

I was chagrined when I quit typing to answer the door recently, but grinned when I saw it was a flower delivery. But no, not for me. The bouquet was for the across-the-street neighbor who wasn't home. With a big old fake smile, I said, "Of course I'll deliver them." But then I knew I'd need to make sure to notice when she got home from work because I was leaving town that evening.

Back upstairs in my tiny office I said aloud, "Now where was I?"

I talked to several authors about this dilemma. One thing for sure: novelists have it rougher than columnists. Wichitan Arlene Rains Graber has written three novels, one non-fictional devotional book and some short stories. Her piece in "Chicken

Soup for Writers" brought a smile to my face because she hit the nail on the head.

In it she wrote about when a neighbor dropped by for a chat. Arlene explained she was working so it wasn't a good time. As the woman gave her a half wave goodbye she cringed. "Just because I work at home – and a writer at that, which no one takes as serious work – doesn't mean my days are empty," she said.

Arlene says writing novels requires "thoughtful, unleashed fabrication." I loved that. She manages to write at home but when it's time for serious editing she heads out of town. She goes back east to a retreat in the spring and goes to various isolated locations in Kansas in the fall.

My friend and author Cheryl Lu Lien Tan who was a fashion writer before becoming an author, goes to a retreat for artists, writers, composers and poets when possible. There she can work without worrying about anything. "They make your meals, all you have to do is work. It's amazing how much you can accomplish when you're not interrupted or distracted," she said.

Another friend and fellow North High grad Janice Graham writes novels. She finds a quiet, somewhat secluded place to live and work far, far from Kansas. She's living in Italy now. When she comes home for a visit we tease her about her tough life. "It's not like I'm in a luxurious villa vacationing," she said.

Authors agree on one thing; it takes discipline to write a book. Some take a year to complete a book, others take longer. Some write three hours a day, others write for eight hours. Some say they write for many consecutive days then take a week or two off.

And I was happy to learn that unlike many newsroom journalists who can write undistracted in the eye of a hurricane, some writers need a quiet atmosphere. They too, give their heads a shake and say to themselves, "Okay, now where was I?"

Oh hey, the mail just came!

The to-do list mentality: Procrastinate, then Panic
August 3, 2014

The old things-to-do list is always there, isn't it? Funny how some things are on the list for days, weeks, maybe even months before finally getting checked off. Those are the things we don't necessarily want to do, and is no immediate need to get them completed.

But do you know when you will get around to them? When there is something that should be done – say, a writing deadline. That's when other things on the list, and even some that aren't on the list, get your attention.

It's such a drag when you've done everything except the most important task at hand. You've prepared dinner (at 2 p.m.), hung a picture that's been leaning against the wall for months, cleaned the drawer that was full of junk. (So that's where the good scissors have been since last year.) All phone calls have been returned and e-mails answered.

The good news is all those things can be checked off your list. The bad news is the task that actually needs attention is lurking there, waiting. Remember in school when you had homework? You did your favorite subjects first. Since I found math a complete mystery that made me cry, I always did English first, social studies next and any extra credit those subjects had to offer. But there was my math, and later algebra, homework, rearing its ugly head. I swear that math book sneered at me, making me wish I had more homework in English.

My mom tried to teach me to prioritize. She always advised doing unpleasant or difficult tasks first. Do prioritize, don't procrastinate. Somehow, I prefer what Mark Twain said: "Never put off till tomorrow what may be done day after tomorrow just as well."

It has been said that creative people are the worst procrastinators. I totally agree with writer Bill Watterson, who said: "You can't just turn on creativity like a faucet. You have to be in the right mood. "What mood is that? Last-minute panic."

Amen to that.

Jazimen Gordon and Bonnie

WSU win proves women's sports have come a long way
March 24, 2013

Progress, growth, improvement. We love to see that and that's one reason I was a laughing, crying, jumping-up-and-down mess when Wichita State University won the Women's Basketball Missouri Valley Conference Tournament in St. Charles recently.

Part of the happy dance was the joy I felt for Jazimen Gordon. I have been her mentor for four years which allowed me to witness her progress as she grew into a fantastic young woman who not only is a heck of a basketball player and a good student, but a caring, funny human being.

I've been lucky to get to know other team members and watched them as they matured under the guidance of Coach Jody Adams and her staff and their mentors.

Sitting in the front row behind the WSU bench I looked at the WSU fans who traveled to St. Charles to support our team. I recalled counting the spectators at a women's game in Henry Levitt Arena in 1976. Fourteen. And that included me, who at the time was assistant to the women's athletic director, and Joe Banks, who oversaw the Arena. The camera man from a local television station would have made 15 but he was there only about 30 seconds. And no, the 30 seconds didn't make it on the news.

Progress, growth and certainly improvement were evident as I thought of how in 1977 Natasha Fife, John Hansan, Sue Bair and I brainstormed on hosting a tournament at Wichita State. Finally, the money was raised (much of it $100 at a time), the teams were invited, and we had ourselves a tournament. Later it became the Pizza Hut Classic. Women's sports have come a long way.

Those of us who love watching women's basketball, volleyball, softball, tennis and track still see inequities, but we must remember 400 or more frequent fans at a game, match or meet is a whole lot better than 14. These women practice hard, train hard and they play hard. They manage school schedules, their sports schedules and they make time to do good things for this community. They deserve our support because they've progressed, grown and improved. And yes, we do love to see that.

Let's skip resolutions and take 2013 one day at a time
January 6, 2013

Putting together a datebook for the new year is my annual moment of reflection. Actually it takes several moments and it's kind of fun. And this time, because I've retired and I am supposed to have less to do, I've downscaled my big book to a much smaller one. That means I'm going to have to copy my address book. No, I don't want to put all that information in my iPhone.

I like paper and pencil. I'm old, and on that subject, old fashioned. If you've been working on your own datebook, checking out your schedule in 2012, you know what I'm talking about when I say, "Good grief, how did I get all that finished?" and, "Holy cow, how my contact list has changed in the last few years." I'm saddened that my friend Jean Garvey is no longer with us. She was one of the women in Wichita who contributed so much to our city. I got a big kick out of her every single time I was around her.

She was without a doubt one of the most joyful people I've ever known. We will miss her. On the bright side of this year's ledger is the birth of my great-niece Ella, who was born on 10/11/12. Her smile is a killer, and all I want to do is sit and hold her and look at her. She'll grow so fast, and because she doesn't live here she'll look different every time I see her.

I've always been close to my niece, Amy, and now she's a mom! Changes. All the time changes. And what about this brand new year we're looking at? Time for improvements! New Year's resolutions are fine, but I make the exact same ones every year. Guess that's something I shouldn't admit, but sadly, it's true. Part of it is my bad timing.

I resolve to lose weight and I do, but then by the end of the year, I have gained it all back so I have to make the same resolution again. I resolve to quit biting my fingernails, and all that works fine until about November when things get really busy and I'm decorating and breaking my nails and, boom, by Christmas I'm putting polish on nubbins. I resolve to work out, and I do, but then other things seem more important, then the holidays roll around again and all that good food and I'm just too full to work out. And that "spending less money" resolution. Well, let's not even go into that.

I still think you should be able to pay your Mastercard bill with your Visa card. This is pitiful, isn't it? At least I'm making you feel better about yourself and your resolutions. Let's just concentrate on the highlights of the year.

For example, what was your most memorable moment this year? What was the biggest surprise of the year? What was the happiest moment? The most embarrassing moment? See? Isn't this more fun than that resolution business? If you've got a great story, write to me. This year we've put up with political bickering, been saddened by the results of weather disasters, and stunned by horrific crimes.

But we've made it to another year. And before you know it another year will fly by and we can make resolutions and reflect on the year, all the time hoping there was more good than bad. For now, let's just take 2013 a day at a time because one thing we know for sure: There will be changes, all the time changes.

Technology isn't nearly as amazing as the human body
October 17, 2021

Don't you hate it when you didn't say something and you really, really wanted to? But the moment passes, and the opportunity is gone.

This happened to me when I overheard three young women in the cosmetic area of Walgreen's talking about how cool their iPhone, computers, iPads and all their other techie stuff is and how they couldn't get along without any of it. One girl said, "It's just amazing how everything you need is on your phone, and the phones get better and better. It's all so amazing."

Their conversation made me think of George Will. Yes, that George Will who is in the Washington Post Writers Group and the author of many, many books. I'm a fan, however I do wish he'd laugh more.

But let me back up here. What I wanted to say to those women was: "All of technology you'll ever see will never be as amazing as the human body and how it functions."

George Will wrote a column in March 2020 about the human body, and I'll never forget it.

He starts out by explaining we worry too much about our health. He quotes Lewis Thomas a physician, philosopher, essayist, administrator, dean of the Yale and New York University medical schools and head of Memorial Sloan Kettering Cancer Center, as saying "we worry too much about our health, as though a human being is a teetering, fallible contraption, always needing watching and patching, always on the verge of flapping to pieces."

Enter, another wildly intelligent man, Bill Bryson, author of the book, *The Body: A Guide for Occupants*.

Since we're all "occupants" I think you'll find this interesting. For example, in the time it has taken you to read this far in this sentence your body has manufactured a million red blood cells that will surge through you every 50 seconds, 150,000 times, which is about a mile or so before in about four months they die. But you don't die, those cells are replaced, brand new and ready to travel.

Bryson says "we are just a collection of inert components." Among them seven billion billion billion atoms. Lots of billions but still not as much as the national debt is it?

And the brain, it might weigh about three pounds, a lot of it is water, some fat and protein, but it's got the latest computer beat hands down. Bryson says even if you're just sitting quietly, doing nothing, your brain in 30 seconds will process more information than the Hubble Telescope has processed in 30 years.

And for me this was a jaw dropper: A tiny piece of cortex, the size of a grain of sand could hold 2,000 terabytes of information. Yes, I had to look up terabyte.

A terabyte (TB) is a unit of measurement in computers and similar electronic devices. One terabyte holds 1,000 gigabytes or a trillion bytes. That little grain of sand size piece of cortex could store every movie and 1.2 billion copies of Bryson's book.

These are just a few of the many amazing facts about the miraculous machine we are occupants of. But our bodies are like computers in some ways. Sometimes it's slow, sometimes it's down, sometimes it needs to just stop, unplug and reboot. But obsessing about our computers or our bodies doesn't solve any tech or health problems.

Good maintenance is the answer.

Time to think about what time means and what it's worth
August 8, 2021

Time out! Let's think about time here for a minute. When I wrote about time last year it was when we were staying home trying to avoid getting COVID and wondering why ZOOM meetings seemed so much longer than in person. But we're still COVID conscious and we're still concerned with time. In a recent conversation with two other women, I was struck by how often the word "time" was used by all three of us. For example, "I don't have much time," and "How much time does it take to bring more coffee?" and "I had a great time." That's when my curious mind took over.

Well, that and I knew I was close to deadline on this column so I asked people what they thought of when they heard the word "time." The first answer came from my husband. He said he thought of the concept of time. Then he launched into a sort of philosophical speech about the passage of time. That's a lawyer for you. Remember when you were a kid and it seemed like forever between birthdays and Christmas? The older you get the faster the time whips by.

Birthdays roll around so fast it's difficult to remember exactly how old you are. When I took my friend Joyce Gregory to lunch we talked about age and I was sure I was a year younger than I am. I told her I simply would not give in and would stick to the age I said and it was one year younger than her. "You're a month older than me! Just keep saying you're that age plus 15 months, then just keep adding months," she said laughing.

Susan Addington said to her the word brings timeless to mind. She said as in timeless classics.

Ruthie Williams says time to her means being on time. No wonder she's such a punctual person. She added, "And it seems there is never enough time." Ruthie retired about six months ago and says that has changed her perception of time.

Kate Miller says if she thinks about time she is reminded of how it seems to fly by.

Then we talked about time well spent. Yes, a refreshing cat nap is time well spent. So is a five-minute break from work, or a long conversation to clear the air between two people. Perhaps then at the end of each day we need to reflect on the last 12 hours to see if most of them were time well spent. Personally, I doubt I'll do that.

If you don't want the answer, don't ask the question. A few days ago my husband and I spent two hours watching a really stupid movie. It was so bad we wanted to see how it ended. Then we were both wondering why we wasted that much time when it could have been well spent. It made me think how often I don't value my time.

Sometimes it's downright frustrating that we can't control time, we can't turn it back or make more of it. Regardless of what comes to mind when you think of time, remember what the very wise Benjamin Franklin said: "Does't thou love life? Then do not squander time, for that is the stuff life is made of." That said, thank you for taking time to read this. Hope you don't think it was a waste of an important commodity, time.

Karla Burns was unforgettable, immensely talented, funny, and kind
June 20, 2021

Karla Burns in *Hello Dolly*

Funerals are thought provoking. And just as my parents once told me, the older you get the more funerals you'll go to. Some have surprises such as the time a daughter got up to speak about her deceased dad and no one knew he had a daughter, not even his second wife.

Oh dear. Talk about a wait…now what? moment.

Funerals are sad because you know you'll not see that person again.

And when that person was a joyful addition to your life it makes it even more difficult.

That's why I cried through a lot of the service for Karla Burns. I loved her dearly. She was an unforgettable, immensely talented, funny and kind person who will surely be missed by many.

Karla would have loved the music, the stories about her that brought laughter and tears. She would have been so pleased to see so many people of all ages, races and religions gathered in her honor. Sitting there holding my Kleenex that was pretty much in shreds, I thought how she would have grinned showing off her gap-toothed smile.

To say she was something special is a vast understatement.

When Karla was young, she got up her nerve and went to New York to audition for a spot in the chorus for the musical *Show Boat*. Instead, she landed the principal role of Queenie. After touring the show ended up on Broadway and in 1984, she earned a Tony nomination for Best Supporting Actress.

After touring with the show in England she was the first African American to receive the Laurence Olivier Award for Best Supporting Actress in a musical.

It was back to Wichita after many years of performing in shows that took her to New York, Europe and Africa. In 2015 I interviewed her for *Wichita Magazine*. Since she was a friend it was an easy, fun interview over lunch. When I asked her if she wanted dessert, she said she was too full but wanted to order one to take home. "I'll think of you later when I'm enjoying this," she said with a wink.

Here are some of my favorite Karla quotes from that interview:

"When I saw *South Pacific*, I thought, Wow! You can do the singing and the acting thing. You could sing in a play! I knew that was something I wanted to do."

"I wasn't the normal, skinny, pretty girl so it was up to me to learn to move this body and shake that thing because nobody is, and I mean nobody is going to shake it for you."

"People say God winks at some people. Well, he has a strobe light going on me."

That's for sure. She was a light in many people's lives, whether she was teaching them to sing, sitting in the audience watching her perform, a fellow cast member, or just a pal spending time talking and laughing.

She talked often about the importance of kindness. But when I asked her what adjective she would like to be used when someone described her, she rolled those big brown eyes, grinned and said, "Magnificent!"

And she was.

The good and the bad of lucky number seven
July 4, 2021

What is your lucky number? Someone asked me the other day what number I considered lucky and I said, "Seven."

Thinking back to grade school (and that is way back) I remember having 7 as my lucky number. Maybe it was because I thought Snow White and the Seven Dwarfs was the best story ever.

Yes, I found the mix of the diverse personalities of Doc, Grumpy, Happy, Sleepy, Bashful, Sneezy and Dopey fascinating. All seven of them. My older brother pointed out I was most like Dopey. I called him Grumpy. He was 10. I was seven.

But siblings and the Disney folks aren't the only ones who have used the number seven.

My in-depth research, oh all right, a quick google peek, revealed the number 7 is mentioned 323 times throughout the Bible.

And let's not forget the Seven Deadly Sins. I found that many people I asked could name all or nearly all of the Seven Dwarfs, but not many of the Seven Deadly Sins.

They are pride, envy, gluttony, lust, anger, greed and sloth. Sloth? I thought that was a very slow animal. It is, but it also means lazy.

When I mentioned the seven deadly sins to my friend Stephanie Tally, she started talking about the movie Brad Pitt was in. But she could name several of the sins and the virtues and did really well naming the Seven Dwarfs.

If we're going to talk sins, we'd better also consider the seven virtues. Can you name them? Everyone seems to remember faith, hope and charity. The other four are prudence, justice, temperance and courage.

Look up those words and you'll also see frugal, fair, and in the case of temperance, habitual moderation of the appetites or passions.

This is where you wonder just how moderate does something have to be before it crosses the line into gluttony or greed. Or does buying your 50th pair of shoes at half price qualify as being frugal?

You see, that's where that moderation business comes in again. All those sins and virtues can get very tangled up and no doubt people can put a huge variety of definitions to each of them.

While looking into the number seven I noticed there were articles and facts about other numbers, ten for example. But who wants to try remembering a list of 10 things regardless of what they are? Memorization doesn't come easy these days.

I still say the best lucky number you can have is seven.

Unless, of course, you're shooting craps.

Let's get to the point, high heels are beautiful, but they can be a real pain
June 6, 2021

The list of things affected by the pandemic is long. One perhaps you haven't thought of, especially if you're a male, is high heel shoes.

Not surprising sales of high-heeled shoes fell 45 percent in 2020. After all, we aren't a bunch of Donna Reeds running the vacuum sweeper in a shirtdress, high heels and pearls.

But we were at home. Home wearing comfy slippers, tennis shoes or flats. Personally, I was barefoot most of the time.

Just think how our feet, lower back and knees rejoiced with the vacation from high heels.

Admittedly I'm a shoe addict. And I do have many pairs of high heels, but I'm finding that I have worn them less and less over the past few years and I have not bought any really high heels in a long time.

It's fun trying them on in the store, looking in the mirror, turning this way and that. You feel tall, long-legged, and maybe even a little sexy. We think: "Wow, these are high and they're still pretty comfortable." We walk around a bit and buy them.

But real life is a killer, just like those shoes are. You wear them to a party where everyone stands around chatting before finally sitting down to dinner. By now you're figuring out how you'll have time to go to the chiropractor the next day. As you sit through dinner your feet are rebelling and swelling. It's as if they're saying, "I'll show you, putting me in these awful pointed-toed stilts. Just wait until you get up and try to walk."

And yet there's something about high heels and the way you feel when you put them on. I have several friends who love shoes as much as I do and they love high heels.

Pamela Ammar, who is an attorney, says for years she didn't feel fully dressed unless she put on a pair of "fabulous stiletto heels." She says it seemed the only fashionable shoes designers created were high heels.

"But fast forward to the last few years and now many designers also create the same, great shoe but with a kitten heel. I'm thrilled I continue to find wonderful shoes in not so high heels," she said.

Cheryl Horton, my friend for several decades, and I have bought many, many shoes together. We've also discussed how some women look simply miserable wearing high heels.

If you can't stand up tall and walk without looking like you're on a tightrope, go for a lower heel. Half the fun of watching an awards show is finding out who can walk with confidence in ridiculously high heels.

"Watching even young actresses hobble on stage takes the glamour out of the overall look," Cheryl said.

It doesn't require a degree in podiatry to know that wearing shoes that put you on your tip toes and those toes are crammed into a pointed shoe, to know it's not good for several reasons. Pain being number one.

My mom used to say "Such price, beauty" when she was giving me a home permanent that smelled awful and burned my eyes. She also said it when I would complain how uncomfortable high heels were, but quickly added she loved how they looked.

The world has never been more casual in the category of clothing. Generally speaking, people are more concerned about being comfortable than being fashionable. No wonder the future of sky-high stilettos is wobbly.

I overheard a woman at a wedding reception say, "My husband loves me to wear high heels. The higher the better. And right now my feet are killing me."

She was wearing a pair of high-heeled sandals made of nothing but multiple thin straps attached to a sole. I almost laughed thinking of what my friend Sally Thompson said about that type of shoe.

"After a while your feet look like one of those big roasts that has string around it," she said.

I tried a pair of high heels on recently that had a "comfort inset." The salesperson said it was much like memory foam.

Memory foam, huh. I already had a pair of high heels with a "comfort insert." The only memory of those shoes was walking down the stairs at the Wichita Art Museum after standing on the stone floor for two hours in heels. Never wore those cripplers again.

Bonnie with Blake and Brock Bell brothers

Wife of a former NFL player, mother of a KC Chief: "I wouldn't trade it for anything"
January 27, 2022

NOTE: When they see the word "Chiefs," in the headline people read the column. This was one of the most well-read columns of mine. Editor Michael Roehrman even put it in the Football Special Section. Go Chiefs!

If you've ever been a teacher, you know how fun it is to talk to a student you had in class decades ago. Especially if that student was fun, cooperative, smart and, all right, I admit it, one of my all-time favorite kids. It was such a treat last week when I had the chance to sit down and catch up with Sherry Bell, a student at Pleasant Valley Junior High in 1970. Of course we talked about the old days, but also what she's up to now.

In a word, football. Blake Bell, Sherry and Mark Bell's son, is a tight end for the Kansas City Chiefs. But football interest started much earlier for Sherry. Before they met, Mark played for the Seattle Seahawks and the Colts. His twin brother, Mike, played for the Kansas City Chiefs.

According to Sherry, if someone asks Mark what it's like to see Blake play in the NFL after being a player himself, he is quick to answer that it's more fun to watch his son than it was to play.

Blake, 30, and his brother Brock, 32, played as youngsters, then both played at Bishop Carroll High School before going to college. "Oh my goodness gracious, I was a sports mom. I cooked meals and made posters," she said. But during their school years it wasn't just football.

"We traveled every summer to baseball tournaments, and they played basketball. Hot summers, sweaty gyms and cold football games. But I wouldn't trade it for anything," she said.

But she does remember the coldest game she ever sat through. "It was at the OU versus Oklahoma State game in Stillwater. Blake came in toward the end of the game and drove them down the field to win the game so it was worth it. But oh, my goodness it was cold!"

Wife, football mom, and now she has a new title: Grandmother. Brock and wife, Lauren, added daughter Brooklyn to the Bell family. Seems the new addition is the star of the family.

"People ask what she's going to call me. I tell them she can call me whatever she wants. And we'll take all the grandkids they want to throw at us," Sherry said. Sherry says Blake's wife, Lyndsay, says she wants to have six kids and two of them twins.

After showing pictures of Brooklyn, it was back to the subject of football. I asked if she worried about injuries. "I've never been a worrier, and I have to just blank it out. I was really more nervous when he was a quarterback," she said.

Blake and brother Brock have always supported each other probably because Sherry says she and her husband made sure they knew from an early age the importance of being part of a strong family unit. "They played lots of sports and were busy growing up, but we sat down and ate dinner together. My boys are really good boys," she said in a very matter-of-fact tone. The first time I met the boys they were in grade school when I asked Sherry if her sons would model for a back-to-school fashion section in *The Eagle*. They were so polite I asked Sherry if she had threatened them.

When Fernando Salazar, the photographer, decided we needed an action shot, the boys were instructed to run and then leap. Already athletic Blake, 8, and Brock, 10, leaped so high only their legs were in the frame. "I saved that paper and showed them the picture recently. I told them, 'See I had you on a career path for modeling, but you went another direction," Sherry said laughing.

On Saturday Mark and Sherry were headed to Kansas City for the game. "You know, it's a lot of effort getting everything organized with the traveling, the tailgating, the game, and then waiting in the parking lot after the game for Blake to come out. It's a long day, but it's worth every minute." The last minute was a long one at last Sunday's game against the Buffalo Bills. To say it was exciting is a vast understatement. "I swear that game took a few years off my life," Sherry said in a phone conversation Monday morning. The Chiefs won in overtime. It will be interesting to see in a few years what sports the Bell grandchildren, who will probably be very athletic, are participating in. "Our kids say they're going to put a golf club in their kids' hands," Sherry said.

If they're golfers, no doubt Sherry will be on the course cheering them on. But she'll have to do it quietly for a change.

New iPhone, new problems – anyone know how to get to the home screen?
March 13, 2022

Well, I finally did it. I got a new iPhone. After friends and family told me repeatedly that I needed a new phone, I caved in and bought one. I must admit the old one needed to be replaced. It didn't function properly probably due its brief swim in the toilet. I name things, so I call my new phone "Pearl." I bought a white one because I thought I'd be able to find it easier in my large handbag with dark interior. Wrong.

This sparkling new iPhone 13 is so far not my friend. It doesn't have a home button. I'm used to that button that seemed to solve everything. The guy at the store who sold it to me quickly said, "It doesn't have a button." At the time, I didn't think it mattered because I'm trainable and there weren't that many phones in stock. I was there, and I wasn't leaving without a new phone. And just so you know, there was no training offered.

When my husband asked how I liked it, I had to admit that I didn't know because I hadn't figured out how to turn it on and get to the home page with all those little squares offering choices of many, many things. What the heck is "Garage Band?"

Anyway, I went online for some tutoring, and it helped. Sort of. It's that swiping thing I'm having trouble with. Pushing a button is much easier. Maybe I should have invested in one of those phones made especially for the elderly. The one with big buttons.

The young man who sold me the iPhone assumed a great deal. He assumed I was good with technology. He couldn't have been more wrong if he tried. When I asked him if he would transfer my contacts to the new phone, he looked at me as if I had asked him to wash my car. But he did it. I for sure wouldn't try anything on my new phone in front of him because, and I'm not proud to admit this, I can't text with my thumbs. I use my pointing finger on my right hand.

But finally, I'm getting better, and I'm trying to remember to delete things after I see them. My last phone had 10,346 emails on it. Honestly, it did. The new one has no emails because adding email to its hundreds of functions is still a mystery to me. By now, those of you who are techies are rolling your eyes and wondering why someone as dumb as I am is allowed to drive a car.

Well, some of us didn't know how to use a mouse before we learned to walk. We didn't have a computer in school or a phone in the fifth grade. I saw a toddler in Best Buy trying to swipe a TV screen that wasn't even turned on. She had the swipe down pat but was obviously puzzled that nothing happened.

But fear not, I'm getting the hang of it. And the Apple folks are tickled to death that I have a new phone. They keep emailing me tips and suggestions on how to use my new iPhone 13. Of course I have to read their tips on my computer. I'll save those valuable tips for after I finally learn the proper technique of swiping, discover how to get rid of apps and take the best photos possible. And who knows? I might even learn exactly what and where the heck the "cloud" is.

Wait. Now what? Don't try to tell me that Shocker fans have no spirit
November 25, 2012

We all have that little saying or thought we say or think when we're sure we didn't hear something correctly. Some might just say, "Huh?" or "What?" Mine happens to be, "Wait. Now what?" I say this when I don't understand something, but also when I am incredulous of something that is said to me.

I have two perfect examples. Not long ago, a man told me there was absolutely no way a university could have school spirit unless it has a football team. At first, I thought he was kidding. Once I realized Mr. Burly Arms was serious, I launched into how Wichita State University fans have plenty of spirit and they fill Koch Arena for basketball games. I'm writing this while I'm in Cancun at the Cancun Challenge. We're here to see both the men's and women's basketball teams compete.

I wish the football maniac was here to see the bleachers full of Shocker fans clad in black and gold showing their school spirit. One couple is here on their honeymoon to see the Shocker games, one man came to celebrate his birthday, and several fans came from across the country to see the Shocks play. We met a couple from Denver who go wherever the Shockers play every Thanksgiving. Also, a couple who moved from Wichita four years ago and now lives in Indianapolis is here.

When I asked men's basketball coach Gregg Marshall what he thought about the large group of fans who came either on the charter plane or on their own, he said, "Shocker fans are loud, they're proud, and they are colorful."

Women's coach Jody Adams said, "Our fans are unmatched. There's a real interest there, and it's on a personal level. Other teams take notice of our spirit. I talk a lot about our environment and how great it is."

Assistant coach Bridgette Gordon said, "Our fans are unique and very special. They don't just watch the games, they know the kids, and the kids know them." So, after experiencing hundreds of Shocker games in my life, it's no wonder when someone said something so ridiculous I said, "Wait. Now what?" My other example was just as upsetting.

I was in a store trying to borrow a shirt that I wanted a handsome model to wear in a charity fashion show. I told the store manager who I was and what I was needing. He said he would have to call his boss. OK, that was understandable. It was the first time I'd borrowed anything from an unfamiliar store since I retired, and it felt weird not to hand him my *Eagle* business card. The young man and his boss wouldn't loan me the shirt because neither one had ever met or heard of me before. Well, OK, that's understandable. I explained I had worked as the fashion writer for *The Wichita Eagle* for 32 years.

"Do you read the newspaper?" I asked. His answer? Get ready. "No, I guess I'm too young." Wait! Now what? I couldn't help myself. I had to say, "You're never too young to know what is going on in your community or to know about the place where you work and live." I handed him the shirt and left. Too young to read the paper? If he thinks it's archaic to hold newsprint in his hands, perhaps he could read it online? I'm sure from time to time I say (or write) something that has a person saying, "Bing, are you nuts?" or "Huh?" or "Wait. Now what?"

And that's good. There's nothing like opposing views to open up dialogue. As author John Powell said, "Communication works for those who work at it." That said, don't tell me Shocker fans don't have spirit or you're too young to read the newspaper. End of discussion.

A lesson from a pop song: Put away your cellphone, and be here now
November 8, 2015

Isn't it fun to find a new favorite song? Mine is "Be Here Now." Not only is the tune by Kenny White catchy, but also the words, by my friend Robin Macy, reflect something I strongly believe in.

I was in my car and slipped in the new Cherokee Maidens CD, *Ride Again*. I liked everything I heard – and then I heard them singing, "I look at your eyes, and to my surprise, I find I'm alone, you stare at your phone." After the part, "Turn off the phone/Take a deep breath/Open your eyes/I gotta confess/Sometimes we forget/To be here now," I yelled "Amen, sister!"

Yes, cellphones have taken over too many lives, but there's more to it than that. We're not looking around, taking it all in. We're not seeing and experiencing our surroundings. We're not looking into a friend's eyes to make sure her heart is feeling what her mouth is saying. Instead, we are seeing the tops of people's heads as they type away.

When I observed a dozen students walking across the bridge by North High, I noticed that each one had earbuds in and was holding a phone. I'm sure they were listening to music, but why weren't they talking to the person walking beside them? It was 75 degrees, no wind, and the trees lining the river are spectacular this time of year. Where were they? Not in the now.

If you find this irritating because I sound preachy, quit reading now because it's going to get worse. You may have noted as a person gets older, some are inclined to enjoy looking back more than being in the present. I remember my mom and I were talking about times when I was in grade school, and she was always a room mother for one of us. We laughed how her three kids kept her plenty busy. She said, "At the time, I didn't realize those were the good old days. But they were. And they were good."

Isn't it going to be hard to call these "the good old days" when we don't remember anything but making sure we get a goofy looking selfie, or an Instagram photo taken? Aren't we going to have memories of picture taking and text messages, instead of the way something really looked, sounded, or felt?

In 1976, I was on a train going through Switzerland, and I remember seeing the Alps, with a valley, the bluest sky and a sweet cottage. It was such a unbelievably beautiful scene that I got tears in my eyes. How lucky I felt to be there to see that. I called my friend Cheryl's attention to it, and she said, "We should take a picture." I told her I'd rather take it all in and remember it. A photo could never be as pretty as the real thing, and I love having it in my memory bank. So many experiences are better in memory rather than online.

About four years ago, I gave the commencement speech at Wichita State. Since then, several students have told me they have reflected on what I said about each day being a gift, and that it's up to you what you do with that gift.

Don't you think our senses are another gift? Shouldn't we use our sight to see things other than screens? Shouldn't we be energized by inhaling crisp fall air? Shouldn't we be hearing voices in person? Shouldn't we be able to eat a meal without a phone in sight? We should eat concentrating on the taste of the food and enjoying the ritual of sharing a meal with others.

It's amazingly difficult for some people to unplug. Dare a person who is constantly on the phone to go cold turkey and leave the phone at home in the underwear drawer. All right, any drawer will do. Better yet, turn the phone off and hide it. You'll be amazed what is offered to get it back.

I asked Robin what inspired her to write "Be Here Now." She said, "Over the course of the past few years, I've observed – with increasing consternation – the way folks are living virtually not necessarily completely." And so I loudly sing along, "Just make a vow, to be here now!"

These clothes really leave nothing to the imagination
January 19, 2020

Are you fascinated with all the technology that is supposed to make our lives easier?

Are you as convinced as I am that sometimes this technology makes life more difficult?

Are you as curious as I am just what this world will look like by the time we ring in 2030?

I've been reading with interest and some trepidation how artificial intelligence is becoming increasingly common in our everyday lives. You don't have to be a scientist to have a robot rolling around your house or have your clothes remind you of a two o'clock meeting.

Wait. Now what?

Yes, I just read an article by Ray A. Smith in the *Wall Street Journal* saying that "data is the new black" in fashion. That's because there can be sensors embedded in the fabric that will monitor how stressed we are, give us reminders of appointments, various alerts and information.

And you thought that Apple watch was hot stuff. Instead of your watch or your phone reminding you of something, the sleeve of your shirt or some part of your garment will glow, blink or vibrate. Oh my, there are SO many smarty remarks that could be written right here, but let's go on.

If you say this won't happen, be aware it already has. According to Rebeccah Pailes-Friedman, author of the "Smart Textiles for Designers: Inventing the Future of Fabrics," much of this technology has been used in the military and in the fields of medicine and sports. She believes blue-collar and white-collar workers are next up to glow, blink or vibrate.

But there's more! Therapeutic wearables. A good example is the "mood sweater" by a company named Sensoree. The sweater has a LED studded collar. It lights up in a variety of colors based on galvanic skin response or a change in the electrical characteristics of the skin. What causes these changes? Stress, of course, but also pleasure, excitement and I would guess anger.

Don't we want something left to the imagination? Shouldn't we continue to look people in the eye to figure out how they're feeling and listen to what they're saying instead of trying to figure out what a pink collar means? Personally I don't want my collar to light up red when I want to poke someone in the nose. It's just best to not telegraph some emotions.

Imagine you're feeling anxious about meeting someone. Before you even shake hands your collar lights up, your right sleeve is blinking and your left sleeve is glowing and you start twitching because something in the middle of your back is vibrating. Talk about wired.

With so many cases of identity theft happening every day, wouldn't it be best to keep at least some thoughts and feelings private?

I would be stunned if any of the data clothes and therapeutic wearables are a big thing in the next few years, but then again it didn't take cell phones long to be what most people consider an absolute necessity.

But for now, data is not the new black.

Castle Used in *Downton Abbey* even more thrilling in person

September. 28, 2014

These days new shows and episodes pack the TV guide, but my all-time, absolute favorite, *Downton Abbey*, won't be back until January. It seems a long time until January. My friends who watch the show think I'm pretty lucky these days because I, old Bonnie from Wichita, America, went to Highclere Castle outside London on September 10. And that's where *Downton Abbey* is filmed. I nearly had a meltdown. It is truly beautiful and so fun to see a place I've seen many times on the television screen.

My husband started watching the show after several episodes had aired so he didn't know that all the scenes I would talk about took place in the hallway we were walking down or what happened early on in the bedroom we were standing in. The castle is now owned by the 8th Earl and Countess of Carnarvon. It has been in the family since the late 1700s.

The interior of the house, which we were allowed to see, is just as it appears on the show. The huge oak staircase is grand. It was fun to see where Mary stood and asked her father how she looked just before leaving for the church to marry Matthew.

From the second floor, you can look down and see the library, where many scenes are shot. Visitors aren't allowed to take pictures inside the castle, but outside I took photos of things I've seen 100 times on *Downton Abbey* episodes.

I rang the doorbell! Oh all right. I just pretended to ring the doorbell. Too bad no one was home.

We also went to the village of Bampton and saw the house that is supposedly where Mrs. Crawley lives. It's next to the church. Yes! The church where Mary got married and Edith got left at the altar looks exactly like that, minus all the flowers that were in the show. This was one of those experiences that, once you're back home, you can't believe you were there. When I started showing my pics to friends, it was interesting to see the difference in reactions of those who watch the show and those who don't. The watchers were excited. If someone asked, "What is *Downton Abbey*?" I knew I better skip to the Paris pics.

I enjoyed seeing the castle and how they changed it to make it work for the show, but then I started worrying. What if seeing it would make watching the new episodes less enjoyable? What if it made reruns less fun? Unable to wait until January to find out, I borrowed my friend Nancy's DVDs and watched.

The first episode had me saying to myself, "Oh my gosh, I was there," and "Look! It's the doorbell. I stood right there!" The giant tree in so many scenes was one of the photos I took. "I have a photo of that wonderful tree!

If you don't watch *Downton Abbey,* you've probably already quit reading or are saying, "Geez, girl, get a life." But if you are an avid fan, you know how thrilling it was. I bought two books about the show and the filming, etc., at the Bampton Library, which is the hospital in the show. The man who sold them to me said he knows that in the upcoming season someone is going to die. Of course, I wanted to know how he knew that, and he said one of the actors on the show told him. He also said that almost every one of the actors is very nice and friendly to the townspeople. No doubt the women in Bampton were happy to hear that George Clooney is going to be a guest star on the show in the new season.

My conclusion is that going to a location makes watching even more fun, and it made me feel even more like I know those people. Seeing the "where" adds to the experience of watching. But seeing the "how" things are done and what goes on behind the scenes takes away a bit of the magic. It was a great experience, and now I can check one more thing off my bucket list. Cheerio! See you at "Downton" in January.

It's all just too much
August 14, 2014

Two words: too much. When a heaping plate of food was put down before my friend at lunch, she said, "Oh, that's too much." Yes, most American restaurants believe in large portions. As we talked about our teenage grandchildren and their love of iPhones, we agreed that in today's world there is too much disconnect. Too much tech talk and not enough face-to-face conversations. Too much texting and not enough touching.

Years ago, it was e-mail that kept us from using our verbal skills, and we wondered what the damage would be. That wasn't nearly the problem that texting is now. People didn't try to type or read an e-mail while driving. No doubt, some people now try using their phones. There's too much looking down at phones while driving. We were amazed when we realized how much of conversation was based around "too much."

For example, kids throw away too much of their school lunches. They have too much homework. They play video games too much. It's not just kids though. A lot of people we know (us included) have too much stuff. Way too much. Are we trying to fill a void? When every drawer, cabinet and closet in the house if full, and then some, isn't it time to say, "Enough!"

It's obvious we're spending too much money on things we don't need. There's even too much stuff in the stores. Too much junk mail comes every day. Too much waste is not being recycled. Too much negativity in political campaigns has voters cringing. Too much entertainment is R rated.

Too much money is coming out of teachers' pockets for supplies needed in their school rooms. Too much abuse is happening to children, the elderly and those who are or feel defenseless. Too much depression is going undetected.

But too much isn't always negative. You can't love your children or your spouse too much. And is there such a thing as too much generosity, too much kindness or too much gratitude? Can you be of too much service to those in need? I don't think so. Some would say there's no such thing as too much money, too much luck or too much time. And many would disagree with one or all of those. Everyone could make their own list of what's too much in their lives.

Today is a good day to think about what changes can personally be made to add a positive "too much" to your life. I'm going to find someone who needs a little help coping with this world we live in, a person who feels like, "It's just all too much."

You have to work at being a good friend to keep your good friends
April 14, 2014

The message said, "It's over."

With those two words, I knew my friend Karla Davison had died. And as my heart sank to the pit of my stomach, I read, "Promises were kept."

Her husband, Joe Davison, kept his promises to her, but Karla, who was diagnosed with pancreatic cancer in October, also kept her promises. She never caved in and asked, "Why me?" Instead, she found joy and peace and love in every day she had left.

She taught us all a lesson in her never-wavering faith. And she made sure at journey's end that Joe would know how to do everything at their home, from sorting and washing the laundry to setting the microwave.

I can't imagine the number of lists she made in her last months. I've lost several friends through the years, but it certainly never gets easier. Each loss reminds me of the importance of friendship. And it's a reminder that friendships have to be nurtured just like any other relationship.

I was only in fifth grade, but I remember having a conversation with my dad about who our best friends were. My answer was Cynthia DeCamp, who lived down the street. I told him, "She's a great friend." That's when Dad said, "You have to be a great friend to have a great friend, and you have to work at it to keep your great friend."

It made some sense then, but now it's crystal clear. All our busy schedules seem to get in the way of "working at it" to make friends a priority. The effort is worth it. At lunch last week, I had a similar conversation with my friend Marni Vliet Stone.

She and I taught at the same school in the '70s and have been friends ever since. We don't get to see each other often, but even if we don't see each for months, we start right in where we left off. When we had one of our April birthday lunches we talked about friendship.

We agreed you have to be a friend to have friends, but it's easy to take close friendships for granted.

But don't.

It can't be said too often: We don't know what tomorrow will bring for us personally, or for our friends. We only can hope for the best, and for best friends.

Moving into a new house is for the birds
November 27, 2022

I've always said, "Never say never." Well, sports fans, I'm taking it back because I am NEVER going to move from one house to another again.

People say it's like having a baby, you forget the pain of moving. One friend even bet me that I'll move again. No, no and no. And I have plenty of reasons why. If you've moved recently and recall the pain, you'll relate.

The first thing I realized is even though we thought we got rid of a lot of stuff, we moved too much. I brought stuff I wish I'd given away or sold and realized things I should have moved are gone forever.

In the process of moving my husband would say "home" and I never knew which house he was talking about. At one point we owned two homes and were not sure where we'd sleep that night.

But here is the first thing that convinced me moving isn't for the weak: First, a little back story. I've been afraid of birds, yes, *all* birds except hummingbirds, since I was two years old. That's when I had an unfortunate and frightening experience with a chicken.

On moving day, as a team of six very strong men carried in furniture and what seemed like a thousand boxes, the front double doors were propped wide open. That's when a HAWK flew into the living room, missing my head by about an inch.

I ran to the laundry room, shut the door, got in the broom closet, shut that door and held it shut with both hands. Hawk extraction was left to my husband and one of the movers.

Standing in the dark I hoped the hawk couldn't find me and also that it wouldn't poop on the brand-new carpet. After a few minutes my friend Roxanne found me and said the bird was gone. She reported it had landed and was shooed out the patio door.

There are other problems. After three weeks we're still trying to find the light switches and there seems like there's a lot of them. We lived in an old house in Riverside where there was only one switch per room. Replacing bulbs in high ceilings and scheduling very busy workmen takes time, but once a project is complete, it's certainly worth it. So far.

The oven makes me long for the days when you simply turned a knob to bake or broil or whatever and then another knob for temperature.

The oven I have now has a Wi-Fi feature. As if Wi-Fi isn't challenging enough? And it's all touch screen. When I finally got it turned on, I couldn't figure out how to turn it off. My friend Lisa Corbin, who is younger and much better with touch screens, agreed it was far more complicated than it should be. Sadly, the microwave also is a bit of a mystery.

And boxes! Holy cow, once they were empty, they took up the entire dining room which was empty because we sold our dining room furniture. Finally, the main floor is looking ok, but the guest rooms and family room downstairs look like a bomb went off.

Lots of drawers and cabinets are opened and closed before we find what we're looking for. After a short time, it's hard to remember just what it was we were after.

I decided when we bought this house and sold our home of 36 years that I would be organized, stay calm and not get discouraged during this transition. Well, that ship has sailed. Major progress has been made in three weeks, but then I look around and a little whimper escapes my lips.

But the neighbors are so nice, the neighborhood has beautiful trees, and we're happy with all the changes we've made to the house. The location is close to almost everything we do.

However, it doesn't feel like home yet, but it will, probably about the time I find where I put my favorite baking dish.

Which adjective would you choose to live up to?
August 7, 2016

When you've been to several funerals in a short period of time, you can't help but wonder what will be said at your own funeral. What adjectives will be used to describe you? What will the attendees hear that will make them nod their heads "yes?"

Then I thought, "forget about after you're gone. How do you want to be described this very day?" I didn't ask people what adjective they'd use to describe me, (I'm not THAT crazy), but what adjective would they want to be described as. And they could say only one.

Several people blurted out an answer, then quickly thought of another one. Some went back to the original answer while others continued to think of new ones. But they had to settle on just one.

"Hmmmmm," said Wayne Bryan. Not quick to answer but he decided to choose "genuine." I would say he's genuine and "invaluable" to Music Theatre of Wichita as producing director.

Lynn Marshall, wife of Wichita State University basketball coach Gregg Marshall, said she hopes she is thought of as a "caring" person. No doubt her family at home and her family of tall young men at Koch Arena would say she's just that.

Al Sanchez, senior vice president marketing at Fidelity Bank, said without hesitation, "celebration." Not an adjective, but he explained, "I think we should celebrate every day. Just about anything can be a celebration."

Clark Bastian, chairman and CEO, also at Fidelity, said, "kind." And that was media buyer Terry Johnson's answer also.

Esther Headley, a marketing research consultant, said she hoped she would be described now and later as "humble."

Homemaker Sally Thompson says she would want to be thought of and remembered as being "joyful." Generous, funny, happy, thoughtful, creative and smart were other answers from many people. Some unexpected ones were "connected," "informed" and "frugal."

Once they had answered, several people asked me what my word would be. I finally decided on "dependable." Bonnie Boynton, who was visiting me from Dallas said it is an "ok adjective, but boring."

I explained that dependability goes beyond doing what you'll say you'll do when you say you'll do it. I think dependable means others can depend on you to be helpful, a good listener, a port in the storm, good for a laugh, generous, understanding, etc.

Then I realized if I want to be thought of now, and remembered that way, I've got some work to do.

Hey! That will work for all of us. Think of your word and if you're not already living up to that adjective, start now.

As the new school year kicks off be thankful for those in the field of education
August 22, 2021

The start of the school year and who knows what this year will bring. We can only hope students will get to sit in classrooms, play in gyms and eat lunch together. This is the time of year when those who are starting into middle school are nervous. Some are very nervous. I know this because a long time ago I was a physical education teacher. It was when there was junior high. Now they go to middle school. I told you it was a long time ago.

I can remember every year on the first day some of the seventh grade girls looked like they might expire before lunch. A combination lock was the bane of their existence. Changing clothes in a locker room the first time nearly sent them around the bend.

At that time they had gone from being the big sixth graders to the little seventh graders. Now they go to middle school so they go from being the big fifth graders to being the little sixth graders. Thankfully in weeks they'll wonder what was so scary. Students, hang in there.

But this year I'm thinking more about the teachers and others in the field of education.

During these pandemic times we have raved about the bravery of health care workers. Yes, the doctors, nurses, first responders, respiratory therapists and everyone in the field of health care deserves kudos because they are essential. We will never forget what they have sacrificed for the care of others.

Teachers also are essential. They have used all their resources to come up with ways to continue to teach and motivate students. And that challenge has had a toll on them.

My friend Roxanne Kellogg was a para at North High School for 14 years. Faced with the possibility of another year like last year she decided to retire.

"When things were normal, I loved it. And this was a very tough decision. But trying to help kids with something like geometry, I didn't feel like I could reach them. It was so frustrating for me and the student. Geometry is a pencil and paper thing. Technology added to the difficulty of every subject every day," she said.

She gave the example of a student who was failing because he wasn't sending in his homework. The problem was he didn't know how to use E-mail to send it.

"I've seen students cry with frustration and teachers too," Roxanne said.

Uncertainty can take the joy out of any situation. And the anticipation and excitement of the first day of school is the perfect example.

As a physical educator I loved seeing the glistening refinished gym floor, the clean lockers in a fresh smelling locker room, and a tiny but spic and span office.

Today would be different because I would stand there looking at the gym floor that didn't see activity last year and wonder if my students would be wearing masks while they took part in physical activity. Or if they would be there at all.

So as the new school year kicks off, be thankful for all those people in the field of education who are making a difference in children's lives and supporting the community.

These people are truly essential.

Travel not for the weak
May 12, 2019

Travel is not for the weak. Truer words were never spoken. My husband and I just returned from Scotland. All the planes were on time, but there were just too many of them.

Security is fun when you have an artificial knee. I get patted down every single time. One woman was feeling my leg and nearly pulled my pants down. All the little challenges aside, it was a good trip. Scotland is beautiful, but the weather was cold. Not chilly, not brisk, cold. And those fields are beautiful green because it rains. Frequently.

My daughter, Susan, gave me a book for my birthday, *Eighty Days*. It's about Nellie Bly and Elizabeth Bisland's history-making race around the world in late 1889. After traveling for 72 days, six hours 11 minutes and 14 seconds, famed journalist Nellie won by a few days.

I'll have to admit she had a much rougher trip than we did returning from Scotland. We were home in a matter of one day - well, 24 hours start to finish.

In Edinburgh, just as we were about to get on the elevator with all our luggage, the fire alarm went off. I didn't want to leave the luggage there, so down the stairs we went.

A strong young man said, "Let me help you with that," and then picked up my suitcase as though it weighed 5 pounds instead of 48. Yes, we had weighed it.

Scottish people are very polite and kind. But don't think for a minute just because they speak English you won't have any trouble understanding them. They speak fast and pronunciation is very different from American speak.

Here are some examples: Hame is home, haud is hold, merit is married, noo is now, oot is out, hing is hang, hoose is house and feart is afraid.

But it was some of the words I really liked such as shoogly, which means shaky and wobbly. A skoosh is lemonade or a fizzy drink, tattie is potato and Peely Wally means pale. Wallies are false teeth, slitter means to spill food on yourself while eating, and a tattyboggle is a scarecrow.

Maw means mum or mom or mother. Which reminds us that today is Mother's Day. Some people may "do yer dinger" regarding this day that honors mothers. That means they will loudly express disapproval, perhaps saying it's a greeting card, retail-driven celebration.

All right, naysayers, don't get the card, the flowers, or whatever - but at least call your mother. At the very least. If she's no longer with us, you'll wish you could call. For the moms out there, have a wonderful Mother's Day.

Oh, and go to Scotland first chance you get.

Growing old gracefully requires a positive attitude
November 20, 2016

A couple of years ago I was asked to speak to a group of women about growing old gracefully. I was perplexed why they thought I should speak on the subject. Yes, I am growing old, but gracefully? Mmmmm, not so much.

Since that time, I've given a revised and re-revised version of the talk a few times. Monday, I had the pleasure of having lunch and talking to the EI chapter of the P.E.O., a group that promotes educational opportunities for women. After I spoke, I asked them to do me a favor: Write down their first name, their age, the age they thought would be considered "old" and what they did to stay young. I couldn't wait to get home to read what they wrote. I'll condense it because it was a good-sized group. And by the way, everyone in the audience was past 60.

The question regarding the age that is considered old brought numbers from 70 to 110. But I liked what Jackie, Elise and Prissy, all 80, had to say. They maintain "old" is always 10 years older than they are. Jackie advises to keep smiling. Elise says it's best to think young and not say, "I'm getting old." Prissy says to be grateful for each day.

Barbara, 73, and Jody, 76, give their husbands some credit. "Enjoying every moment and loving each and every day I have with my husband" is what Barbara says keeps her young. "A happy marriage. Marriage is not 50/50, it is 100/100 percent. And you get it in return," Jody said.

The power of positive thinking was written on several cards.

These women were so positive and upbeat I left there inspired and smiling. And they weren't even drinking wine. Barbara, Marilyn, Elizabeth and Rebecca, ranging in age from 62 to 81, said their faith helps keep them young and positive.

Several women mentioned the importance of keeping your body and mind active. Mary, 88, said to read and do things that are worthwhile. Beverly, 79, said to read, but also do crossword puzzles, and have an interest in people young and old.

Volunteering was another suggestion. Debbie, 61, says she thinks old is around age 75. I bet she'll change that number about the time she hits 70. But she says it helps keep her young to mentor young adults in their 20s who are coming out of homelessness.

Exercise, especially walking, was written on several cards. Christie, 65, advises eating more fruits and vegetables. Georgia, 90, says to stay young you must "eat properly and exercise regularly." She appears to be doing just that.

These ladies told me they cherish long friendships and enjoy making new friends. And of course, they commented on the importance of family.

If you're past the age of 40 none of this is big news, but it was fun to see a group of philanthropic women who come together regularly for a meal, a meeting, and a whole lot of fun.

When my next birthday rolls around it's a "biggie," as my mom used to say. That day I'm going to stay away from my magnifying mirror, have a positive attitude, and smile all day. It's been proven you look younger when you smile. My mantra will be "age is just a number." Time goes faster and faster with no way to slow it down. So, let's just laugh. At least laughing, sometimes at ourselves, will keep us young at heart.

Be thankful, even though the world seems very wobbly and out of sorts
November 15, 2020

Can you believe Thanksgiving is next week? With this pandemic keeping almost everyone at home more than usual you'd think the weeks would crawl by. But noooooo. It's almost turkey time and that means family. Usually.

Oh for the old days. Uncle Harry shows up smelling like he started celebrating at 6 a.m. Brother-in-law Dan has been working out so he is the one who motions for Mom to hand him the pickle jar that he'll open with no strain. And he finally does.

At dinner cousin Alvin eats most of the mashed potatoes before everyone gets their first helping. But it's Aunt Pam, who is never satisfied with the conversation until she can start a verbal political brawl. This conversation is even louder than when one sibling says to another, "And just what do you mean by that?"

It's going to be very different this year. How can we possibly do all of the above effectively if it's a virtual gathering? If we could get everyone on House Party or Zoom, and that's a big IF, it would be something like this: Yes, we would probably hear Granny's dentures clacking and the kids belching contest. We'd see Uncle Harry dozing off after his eighth glass of wine and Mom trying to get everyone to eat more. But of course, it still wouldn't be the same.

At the table it may be just immediate family, or maybe family and friends, perhaps just friends. Regardless who the diners are you're going to have to keep your distance and wear a mask except of course when you're consuming more calories in one day than you've had in the past week.

Some people I've talked to are going to have Thanksgiving dinner for only those who live in their houses and then call relatives later in the day. No matter what your plans are it's a day to be thankful. Be thankful if you're healthy. Be thankful if you've been ill and now you're well. Be thankful, even though the world seems very wobbly and out of sorts.

I've never seen a time when it's been so difficult to be thankful and positive. Especially positive. There's pandemic pessimism going around and it seems to be sucking the joy out of our lives. But only if we let it. Now, raise your right hand. You're not doing it. Come on now. All right now read the following aloud:

I promise from now until Thanksgiving Day every day I'm going to name three things that I'm thankful for. No repetition please.

I'm going to find joy and comfort and help others do the same. I'm going to play music and dance around with or without a partner. Yes, seriously.

I'm going to get up and move when I feel lethargic or depressed. I'm going to refrain from starting Thanksgiving Day the way Uncle Harry does. I'm going to brag on the cook or cooks who prepare the Thanksgiving meal no matter how many TUMS I have to take.

There. Now you can put your hand down. Let's keep those promises! And have a wonderful Thanksgiving.

Going to the Emmys a dream come true for this Wichitan

September 24, 2015

Yea! One more thing crossed off the old bucket list. I have always wanted to attend an awards show, especially the Oscars or Emmys. So you can imagine I was just a little bit excited when my friend Sierra Scott got two tickets to the Emmys, and her fiancé didn't want to go. And bless her heart, she asked me.

If you watch Sierra on the "Brett and Sierra Show" or are a friend of hers on Facebook, you already know the trip was really fun. The woman was snapping photos and posting something every time I turned around. And since she has a gazillion Facebook friends, the word went far and wide.

Personally, I am flunking Facebook. I look at it about every other month and don't post a thing.

My traveling companion, who is the only person I know who takes more shoes on a vacation than I do, went to the Emmys last year so she knew the lay of the land. We had the perfect spot in the hotel lobby to watch for stars. She found out the Property Brothers from HG-TV were in the house and went on point. When she spotted them, she covered 50 feet in spike heels in a few seconds flat. I wished I'd had a stop watch.

Of course, the photo of us with Jonathan and Drew Scott is really good of everyone – except me, who wasn't sure what was going on. Nothing new there. Here it was 4 o'clock in the afternoon, and people were dressed in evening gowns because they have to be in the theater by 4:30 or they don't get in.

Let me tell you it was a hot day in L.A. The Microsoft Theater was cool, but the long walk on the red carpet wasn't. We weren't on the same red carpet as the stars, but we were on a red carpet. It was maybe the best people-watching on Earth.

People in the television industry take this day seriously, but most of them seem to have a fine time. Jon Hamm dazzled his biggest fan. Me. I thought it was great that he crawled up onto the stage.

We had pretty good seats in the loge area of the Microsoft Theater, but you do see everything much better at home on your sofa. Part of the excitement of being there is during the commercial breaks when the first three rows look like a fire drill. They move nominees for the next categories up so it won't take them long to get to the stage if their name is called. People who were just onstage have time to get back to their seats, and on it goes. You could tell when someone in our section had worked on a show that won because they would jump to their feet and hoot, holler, hug and high-five.

But the trip wasn't just about the Emmys. On Saturday, we decided to go full-tilt tourist and get on one of the hop-on, hop-off buses. We went to Beverly Hills. We went to Hollywood.

Did you know a couple from Kansas started the area now called Hollywood? Sierra and I about fell off the top tier of the bus when we heard that.

We strolled down Rodeo Drive where we saw a Shocker-yellow Bentley in front of the Bijan store. It had its own yellow parking meter. You have to have an appointment to shop there. We took a pic of the car and moved on.

It was fun to go into the hotel where *Pretty Woman* was filmed. By that time, a cold glass of champagne was in order. Sadly, Richard Gere wasn't there to pick up the tab, but we did love seeing the red dress that Julia Roberts wore in the movie. We didn't have much time to shop, but we did manage to purchase boots and shoes (what a surprise) before heading to the airport.

Once on the plane, we both started looking at our day planners and knew it was time to get back to the real world. But we agreed landing at our new, beautiful airport made re-entry much easier.

Handling bad situations with grace
August 6, 2017

The young woman never looked me in the eye or in my direction for that matter. She didn't say a word. She dropped my purchase in a sack and shoved it out of her way. I picked it up, said, "thank you" and walked out the door wondering how she keeps her job.

It's not just people my age wondering where courtesy has gone. We've missed the bygone concept of customer service for a long time, but when did kindness and being courteous become a thing of the past? Sitting at the stoplight on my way home I was still thinking about the teenager at the cash register. I didn't accelerate the second the light changed so the person behind me honked. I hate that. It was two seconds instead of one before I moved and the guy is honking. I thought, 'Geez, why is everyone acting like they need more fiber in their diet?' I wondered if the heat was getting to these grouchy folks who have the "I hate my life" expression on their faces.

At the next stop light I could hear my mom saying, "Take a look from the other side."

All right. Maybe the teenager at the cash register just had a heart-wrenching break-up with her boyfriend and she thought life as she had known it with Mr. Wonderful was over forever. Maybe her grandma is sick. Maybe she can't bear the thought of summer being over.

Maybe the guy at the stop light was trying to get to the hospital because his wife just texted she is in labor. Maybe he was late for an important meeting with his boss. Who knows.

I can't help but wonder if some of this age of rudeness comes with the tsunami of technology. Are we really more concerned with what shows up on our phones than the look on someone's face? Perhaps someone who needs some undivided attention? Not to mention it is much easier to be rude, and yes, downright mean, when you can type it instead of saying it.

I've learned it's not wise to write something very negative and immediately hit "send." Wait. Breathe. Sleep on it.

I've seen things escalate pretty quickly when someone starts shoving in a crowd or cuts in line. It's not always easy to close your eyes, take a breath, and "go to your happy place" when at that moment it would feel so much better to say, "Hey, (fill your favorite bad name in here) who do you think you are?"

Don't you think the more stressful your day has been, the worse you are at handling someone's rudeness? And stress tends to make anyone more short tempered than they would be on a good day.

I've often thought it would be nice to change the "every man for himself" mentality to "we're all in this together." Because we are.

We see politicians being anything but civil to each other and continually hear complaints from people who can't see beyond their own needs and wants. So we shouldn't be surprised that handling bad situations with grace is no longer the norm.

I'm following my mom's advice she gave me when I was a seventh grader when a friend hurt my feelings. I'm taking a look from the other side. Sometimes it works. And, well, sometimes not so much. But we have to try.

Smile like you mean it, you mean it, you'll feel better
May 13, 2018

Quick, name three people you know personally who have great smiles. No, you don't know Julia Roberts personally, but she does have a wonderful, very big smile.

The first person that comes to mind for me is my mom. Even as a child I remember people telling mom she had a great smile. Maybe it was because it was a genuine, big smile, or maybe it was because she lived her whole life in Kansas.

Many people who visit Kansas say they're surprised how many people smiled at them while they were here. Good for us. And in those, "here let me hold the door for you" situations, a semi-fake smile will work. But who knows the difference between a fake and a genuine smile? Everyone. We may not spend more than a nano second deciding if a smile is coming from the heart, or just from an upward curved mouth, but so many times it's obvious.

An episode of *The Good Doctor* got me thinking about this. It was explained the way you tell a genuine, heartfelt smile from a fake is activation of certain facial muscles. When I looked it up the muscle is the orbicularis oculi which is around the eye socket. This brings to mind the quote, "Let my soul smile through my heart and my heart smile through my eyes, that I may scatter rich smiles in sad hearts."

My granny put it another way: "Go through life grinnin,' you'll feel better and so will everyone else."

I'm a strong believer in smiles and laughter. We've all had those days where you have to smile until you mean it, but once the crevice between your eyebrows relaxed and your frown was upside down, didn't you feel a whole lot better? And that smile can make a statement without saying a word. It's been said that a smile is a universal language. I haven't been all over the world, but it's been true the places I've been. If you smile and mean it, a person will forgive you for not knowing their language.

Mother Teresa was a big believer in smiles. Two favorite quotes from her: "Every time you smile at someone, it is an action of love, a gift to that person, a beautiful thing." And another one: "We shall never know all the good that a simple smile can do."

Have you noticed you smile a lot when you're around children? In an article about what happens to your brain when you smile, researcher Dr. Sayed Atalla refers to a study about the number of times a person smiles. He says we feel happier around children because they smile more. On the average, they smile 400 times a day. Happy adults smile 40 to 50 times a day, but he says the average person smiles only 20 times a day.

Now that last part is just sad.

And here's a little something for you guys to think about. According to another study from Dr. Atalla's research, women smile more than men and women are better are detecting a fake smile.

Back to the three people you named with great smiles: How many were women? Regardless, tell them the next time you see them they have a great smile.

Tomorrow is Monday so just go out there this week and exercise your zygo-maticus major muscle that controls the corners of your mouth and your orbicularis oculi, which will show off your crow's feet.

After all, your smile is the most important curve on your body.

Rockettes' job not just for kicks
August 16, 2010

Four attractive young women were kicking around Wichita last week. And they've got a job many dream of.

Mary Capellas, Christina Cichra, Kate Vallee and Jessica Osborne are Rockettes. They were in Wichita promoting their Radio City Christmas Spectacular that will be in Wichita at Intrust Bank Arena in November. Not only are they pretty and they can dance, but they also are so fun to talk with that it was difficult to keep the interview to an hour.

Mary, originally from Warren, Ohio, who has been a Rockette since 1999, said she has several funny stories but her favorite is the tuba story.

"We were doing the rag doll number- and we were wearing the shoes with the cute little green bows. I'm kicking, and my shoe flew off and went in the orchestra pit *into* the tuba," she said. "It was like a three-point shot in basketball!"

All four have been dancing since they were 3 years old, and each decided they wanted to be a Rockette before the age of 10.

The mention of the Macy's Thanksgiving Day Parade where the Rockettes are featured every year brought big smiles.

"It's wonderful! It's freezing cold, and you don't even care," Mary said. She said it's also cold when they perform at the holiday tree lighting in Rockefeller Center in early December, but that doesn't bother them either.

"It's packed just like Times Square on New Year's Eve, and everyone is in the holiday spirit," Christina said. All four say they're proud to be a Rockette because of the fine tradition and reputation the troupe has.

It's all about precision, beauty and, like so many girls, I wanted to be a Rockette. I did what I thought were high kicks all through high school and college.

But then before a person goes off to New York City to audition to be a Rockette, she should take note of a few restrictions.

You have to be at least 18 years old. Check. (There's no limit to how old you can be!)

You need to be between 5-foot-6 and 5-foot-10½ tall.

Check. You must be congenial and supportive of the other dancers with your Rockette family. Check.

You have to be able to dance really well, smile big and be pretty. Uh oh.

And your kick. It's got to be "eye high." Okay, never mind.

The famous kick line is precision plus. These dancers explained that if everyone in the line kicks eye high, no matter how tall you are, it looks like everyone is kicking the same height because the tallest dancers are in the middle.

Well, all right, I was never a Rockette, but I know the secret of the kick line, and now you do too.

What do interesting people have in common?
Purpose
October 31, 2021

Isn't it great to meet interesting people? People who have ambition, imagination, goals, determination and dreams? They're the ones I'm talking about here.

This was a week filled with interesting people. By Wednesday it dawned on me the more interesting people you know, the more interesting people you'll get to meet. Here's proof: Thanks to one of the nicest and most energetic people I know, Roy Heatherly, I met Conner Hampton. He's a young man who is going to raise the money to build Center City Academy, a beautiful day care facility downtown where children from infancy to five years old will be safe and educationally enriched at an affordable cost to families from diverse backgrounds.

I have no doubt he'll get it done with the help of our generous community. The next day I had the pleasure of meeting Dr. Larisa Genin, dean and professor at the W. Frank Barton School of Business at Wichita State. She told me about plans for the business school that go far beyond the new facility.

My friend for decades, Christa Rude Vazeos, got us together for coffee for a too-brief but very informative time. Here's another revelation: Know what interesting people have in common? Purpose. Next time you hear someone say "purpose," check how they're using it. Purpose is what I call a "stretchy" word. It can mean many things.

I associate purpose with ambition, energy, and a goal. Some would say it's simply a "reason" for doing something. But it's more important than a reason. The reason you put gas in the car is so it will go. But you go for the purpose of doing something.

Maybe it's to help someone, or to achieve a task. When I asked a friend how his daughter was doing, he frowned and said, "She's OK I guess, but she's not really doing anything." After we chatted it was evident the young woman needed a purpose, something to reach for, an accomplishment that would lift her spirits and self-esteem When I said this to her dad his face lit up and he said, "Yes! She needs a purpose, something to get up for in the morning." Without purpose, inertia sets in. And it's a mental and physical place that's not easy to get out of. Like many others I've talked to since COVID, I learned the less I do, the less I do. But it has slowly returned to the more I do, the more I do.

It's important to be grateful, and several times I've thought how glad I am to have purpose in my life, whether it's the importance of my family, a cause, a mission, or a desire to make changes for the better. I read somewhere that if we realize our purpose in life, it's easier to see who we are and why we're here. After all, we are taking up space on this planet. And I'm convinced if we surround ourselves with people who have purpose in their lives and understand the importance of it, we'll find them interesting and that makes us more interesting. And shoot, who doesn't want to be more interesting?

Wonderful Memories
April 24, 2022

We've all had them. Those "Hmmm, I wonder if all this is worth it" moments Travel these days and I guarantee you'll have those moments. So many of them they may even add up to an hour. Or two.

We had planned a trip to Italy in 2021, but of course COVID changed that. We postponed it until March and then into April this year, knowing that masks and shots and having a cotton swab tickling your brain would all be over by now.

We were wrong, but we jumped through all the hoops of getting a health card, being tested no more than 72 hours before boarding a plane, etc. Our friends and neighbors, Paula and Gary Weber, took us to the airport.

A mere 15 hours later we were in Florence renting a car and still wearing our masks.

We hadn't been in the land of pasta and pizza an hour before discovering a passport had been lost and a driver's license was about to expire. We got in the car and headed to the place we rented.

Things were going all right until the navigator (me) told the driver (my dear husband) to turn left because the other way looked like a driveway. Wrong. In a matter of minutes we were lost in the hills. The scenery was great, but a little sleep on a nice bed sounded better than sightseeing.

Thanks to Matteo, our new friend who was at the villa, we finally found our home for the next three weeks. It was even better than the photos we had seen online, and the people who owned it were the most gracious hosts you'd ever hope to find.

It's true not knowing the language can be frustrating. We finally figured out the parking meters and the self-service train ticket machines. As a matter of fact, I helped an Italian woman with the parking meter machine the day before we left. I was so proud.

We spent two days in Florence before coming home. Parts of the city were very crowded, and it was so different than being up in the hills. But I lucked out when I found a great hotel on the Arno River where we celebrated Dick's birthday.

We had to get up at zero-dark-thirty to get to the airport to come home. Caught that plane to Munich, caught the next plane to Chicago. Piece of cake.

Got to Chicago at the same time another, or maybe two, huge planes arrived. We had to go through customs. Note to self: Everyone now has TSA pass.

There we were in the longest line I've ever been in. This line made the Disneyland Matterhorn line look like nothing.

You know how the airport line snakes around, walking and walking, stopping and stopping? Well, there were so many people they had us snaking in all areas including a wide hallway. I looked behind us and could not see the end of the line.

When we rounded the last corner and had eight people to go before it was our turn, a young man in front of us ducked under the tape and got ahead of those 8 by doing so. What a jerk! Karma will catch up with him.

After we got our bags and took them to the transfer area so they'd end up in Wichita. An attendant looked at our boarding passes and said, "Nope, you're not going to make your flight, go to the ticket counter."

This was most definitely one of Those Moments. The first attendant needed corrective lenses badly as she leaned forward and squinted to see the screen. Her vision wasn't the only problem. It was obvious she didn't have a clue what to do with us.

At least she asked for help. There was not a single plane on any airline going to The Air Capital until the next morning.

The I Wonder Moments were piling up at this point and I was hungry. Deep breath. Don't cuss. At least you're in the United States.

Once we got everything organized and ate a little dinner, Dick and I talked about how fortunate we are to get to travel. We agreed our problems on the trip were absolutely nothing compared to people in our world today who have been driven from their homes, lost loved ones, and have no idea what the next day will bring.

We arrived in Wichita the next day. The Webers picked us up at the airport. Paula had put together a basket of stuff for our lunch and our breakfast because she knew we didn't have groceries and wouldn't want to go to the store. What a nice homecoming.

When we told them of some of the hiccups on the trip, they looked like they wanted to ask, "Did you yell at each other? Was it all worth it?" No, we never did yell, and yes, YES, it was all worth it.

The passport was found, the driver's license renewed. Looking at photos from the trip makes moments of frustration fade, replaced by wonderful memories.

Take a minute...

It's fun to ask someone what their earliest memory is. What is your earliest memory? Most people I've talked to say their first memory was around age 2 or 3. Here's an exception.

My friend Stan Rogers claims he remembers being in the womb. Now before you laugh, I remember reading about memory and several people in the article claimed the same thing.

"It's an odd thing, but I swear I remember," he said. So I asked, exactly what does he remember. "It was warm and comfortable. Sometimes I could hear sounds and once in a while I could see light," he said. But he doesn't remember being born. Go figure.

Several told me their first memory involved pain. Jazimen Gordon said she remembers her uncle's old dirty truck. "The kids all rode in the back. I wasn't out there when they started driving off so I ran and jumped on, but my leg hit the exhaust pipe and I got a big, bad burn."

Annie Garvey got bored while riding in the car with her family. She got off her grandmother's lap, jumped over the seat where her brothers were fighting, and proceeded to open the door and jump out. "The next thing I remember is waking up in the hospital crib and Mother walking away," she said.

Jane Knight remembers jumping on her parents' bed and ended up with a broken collar bone. "It was summer with no air conditioning and I had long hair. I remember being told that because the cast covered so much of me, I couldn't take baths, and it was so hot," she said. She was around 3 years old at the time.

But sometimes it's laughter that prompts a memory. Pamela Ammar remembers at about 2 years old her dad would pick her up by the front of her sleeper and drop her on the bed. "I would laugh. I remember I had a white chenille bedspread," she said.

Brief encounters with strangers also are earliest memories for some people. My earliest memory was when I was 2 years old. My mom and I were taking the train from Kansas City to the Mayo Clinic in Rochester, MN. Still in the station I stood up on the seat and looked out the window. There was a train on the next track. A pretty lady saw me and smiled. I waved just as her train started moving and she was gone. I guess I remember her because she seemed so nice.

Needless to say family and siblings are in a lot of first memories.

My husband's first memory is seeing his dad walking toward him on the sidewalk carrying his suitcase.

Tom Shine says he remembers a family portrait when he was 3. "I remember the photographer unloading all his gear for a photo session at our house. He posed us on a bench," he said.

Adriene Rathbun says her first memory was when she was 2 years old. She was twirling around staring down at her Miss Piggy shoes while her dad and brother were playing ball.

Sheryl Wohlford was not yet 3 years old but remembers her brother trying to chase her in his walker with wheels.

Then, there's my brother, Dale, who claims: "My first memory is being in my baby bed and my sister stealing my baby bottle.

"Well, maybe not the last part but I'm sure it probably happened," he said with a snicker. Some things never change.

It's easy to hear stories so many times that pretty soon it seems a vivid memory instead of a story. But there's usually no harm in that. Notice I said usually.

Memories are what make up our life story. Whether it's your earliest memory or something that happened last week, it's now part of you. Memories can be fun, painful, fleeting, sweet, sad, and many other things, but they're yours and stored in your memory bank. And if we're smart, we've learned from our memories.

Take a minute and think of your earliest memory. You might ask yourself, 'why do I remember that?' Then think of five wonderful memories from any age. Now share them with someone.

I hope it will make your day.

Fifth grade girls agree: there are too many guns out there
December 23, 2012

If you're reading this, it means the Mayans were wrong. The world didn't end Friday. I figure the Mayans those many years ago decided figuring a calendar to 2012 was plenty long enough. At any rate, we're still here. And the ones who aren't are being mourned.

In a way the world did come crashing down for the residents of a tiny town in Connecticut. A horrific event that delivered an excruciating punch in the gut to that community. A jolt that was felt across our entire country. And the pain remains. And certainly not only with adults.

I have lunch with a group of terrific fifth-grade girls every Tuesday. I've done this for years, but this is an especially good group. We start each session with "highs" and "lows." Sure enough, one student said her low was "the awful murders in that little town. Those were little kids," she said. She seemed to know more details than I wanted her to share with the group about the horrific incident.

The subject kept coming up as we went around the table, so I decided to ask, "What do you think can be done to keep this from happening again?" One girl said, "I don't know, but we had a lockdown this morning. And I was scared." It was true. The school office had been contacted that morning to go to lockdown because there was a suspicious character in the vicinity of the school. "We need to illegalize guns," the well-informed girl said. "If only the police had guns, then regular people would quit shooting each other."

"Regular people don't shoot people. They shoot birds and stuff," was one response.

The statement "The bad people shoot people. And the crazy people do, too," brought a discussion of whether all bad people are crazy and if crazy people are all bad.

There was not a consensus; most of the girls thought it would have to be looked at case by case. But they did agree there are too many guns out there, and that "crazy people should not be allowed to buy guns."

By the way, these girls have given gun control a lot of thought.

The little girl who was killed in September by a drive-by shooter while she slept in her bed had been a third-grader at this school. We finally got off the subject and had our Christmas party and talked about what we wanted for Christmas. It ranged from a Kindle to "having dinner with my whole family with no fights."

They left wearing the matching necklaces I gave them along with the red ribbon I had used on the wrapping. Their spirits were high, wishing me "Merry Christmas" and giving me extra-big hugs. Last girl out the door turned and said, "One more thing for Christmas, Miss Bonnie: No more shooting. They have to quit."

Yes. Yes, they do

Successful Wichita natives praise their schooling here
February 26, 2012

High schools turn out graduates every year not knowing what they will do or where they'll end up. Some graduates, however, are easy to follow or find because they've become famous. I went to North High School in Wichita and I'm sure I had the very same hall locker as the very beautiful actress Vera Miles. Or maybe it was the same one used by Barbara Sinatra. Yes, both went to North.

It's true: Knowing that famous people graced the halls of your high school is a point of pride. I think I got a good education at North. I mean, there is only so much you can do with a student who is missing the math chip in her brain, but I felt prepared to go on to Wichita State. At North I was crazy about my English classes and physical education. I remember the struggles and the fun.

It's easy to remember teachers who taught us lessons not only about the subject they taught, but about life as well. But what about those very impressive grads from local high schools who put Wichita on the map with their enormous accomplishments? Did they think they got their money's worth from USD 259? I wondered about those who went into acting such as Kirstie Alley, who graduated from Southeast in 1969, Don Johnson (South, 1967) or Karla Burns (West, 1972). Burns, who was nominated for a Tony Award for her role in *Showboat* on Broadway and who has sung and acted in hundreds of shows, says she loved her days of being a West High Pioneer. "Especially my senior year. I only needed one class to graduate – government," she said.

But she didn't want to graduate early. "I wanted to stay where there were teachers with so much knowledge. They influenced me and convinced me I could do well for myself if I applied myself," she said. Burns took government, but the rest of her classes revolved around music and drama, she said. She loved playing the clarinet in the band and was first chair in the orchestra.

She was happy the instrumental teacher, Charles Emmons, came to West from her junior high, Roosevelt. She remembers the drama teacher, Nancy Lackey, fondly. "I thought she was *gorgeous* and she had so much knowledge of the theater. She was one of the reasons I started doing theater." And the vocal music teacher, Sue Hiebert, has a special place in her heart.

"Miss Hiebert told me 'You can sing, kiddo,' and before that I had planned on being a math major," Burns said. "When I look back on those days, I remember the teachers being dedicated and loving what they did. And with the knowledge they gave me I was ready to go on from my high school experience," she said.

Athletes such as basketball star Antoine Carr, who graduated from Heights in 1979, have never forgotten their roots, and that's true for football great Barry Sanders, a 1986 North High graduate. Sanders says he has many memories of North and not just because he went there.

His parents went to North, his 10 siblings went there, and more cousins, nieces, nephews than he can count went to North. "I have great memories of the kids that I grew up with in sports and other activities. It really was a home away from home for me," he said. Sanders was homecoming royalty, crowned Pigskin Pete in 1986, and became professional football royalty winning the Heisman Trophy in 1988. He says he stays in contact with some high school friends.

"In fact, one of my closest friends, Mark McCormick, co-wrote my autobiography with me," he said. Sanders says he liked all his teachers and felt they genuinely wanted him to succeed. "But the one faculty member that impacted me the most was Coach Burkholder. He was so positive and motivational. He taught me so many lessons. I don't think I can ever thank him enough."

Sanders remembers suffering through English, mainly when he had to read Shakespeare and "trying to figure out the message of the books." His favorite subject was math, specifically geometry. "North really prepared me for college at Oklahoma State. I always tried to be a good student and I learned a lot of my study habits that served me well in college in the library at North," Sanders said.

Robert Gates, secretary of defense from December 2006 to July 2011, is a 1961 graduate of East High. He worked in the CIA for 26 years before being appointed by President George W. Bush. After graduating from East he attended William and Mary College in Williamsburg, Va., on a scholarship. He is now chancellor of William and Mary. He was inducted on that school's 319th anniversary on Feb. 3.

"My favorite subjects at East were history and science, but I remember my English composition teacher, Nell Westcott. She taught me how to write," he said. And although he wasn't an athlete in high school, he remembers fondly coach Bob Timmons. "I worked for him for three years as a team manager. In those three years I never heard him swear at a kid, or swear at all," he said. "He was a great role model."

This very high-profile Blue Ace turned down President Bush when he was offered the post as secretary of the newly created Department of Homeland Security. But he didn't turn down the opportunity to talk about his high school education. When asked if he thought he got a good education at East High, he said without the slightest hesitation: "Absolutely. When I went to William and Mary, I was competing against students who came from prep schools and private schools in the East, but I felt very prepared for college."

We can only hope if students are asked about their education in 20 or 30 years, they'll be as positive as Burns, Sanders and Gates. As a graduate of a Wichita high school and a former teacher I have to tell you what I have always believed.

A good teacher is an invaluable part of society, but it continues to be the responsibility of the student to get an education. High school years are a special time in a person's life, and I was happy to hear that three out of three very accomplished people say their Wichita high school educations played a role in their success.

There's no going back after it's too late
July 3, 2016

"And now it's too late." How many times have you said that sentence that is filled with regret? Maybe you've put off picking up a prescription from the pharmacy until it was too late because it closed, or you delayed putting a bid on a house that was sold out from under you.

Muttering "now it's too late" happens for a number of reasons, from not taking the hamburger out of the freezer in time to cook it for dinner to having your insurance canceled because you didn't pay the premium. But sometimes it hurts more than that.

My friend since the eighth grade, Bobbie Harris, moved from Wichita to Shell Knob, Mo., a few years ago. She came back to Wichita from time to time, and some of those times I got to see her.

Any time we e-mailed, texted, talked on the phone, or had lunch, she would insist I come see her. She wanted me to see the improvements on her house that were finally complete. She was obviously proud of her home. I told her I'd love to come see her and hang out for a few days and I would do it. Soon.

I finally went to Shell Knob last week, but it was for Bobbie's funeral. She was killed in an accident just a few days after she'd been to Wichita. I'm having a difficult time believing I won't be getting an e-mail soon or sending her birthday card in August. Now I wonder what I was doing that was so important that I couldn't go visit her.

She had made many friends and wanted me to meet them.

I'm sad I met them when she wasn't there to introduce us. I finally saw her house and wished I could tell her how great it looks.

As my mom got older, she constantly encouraged me to "do it now." "Do it while you can," she would say. We may have been talking about travel, doing a good deed, or taking on a new challenge. Regardless, she would tell me to "do it now."

If I could turn back time, I'd go to Shell Knob, and my friend and I would talk and laugh about the many chapters in our lives we shared. We'd laugh and talk about books, movies, mutual friends and the many changes that come with age. It would be a fun visit that I could reflect on. I know I would have been glad I had taken the time and effort to go.

But instead, I am reminded of an important life lesson: Do it now. My friend wanted me to come for a visit. And now it's too late.

After 30 years it's time to slow down
April 30, 2012

It seems word is out: I am retiring. When people I don't know walk up and tell me what they think of this decision, I guess it's time to make it official. I've been typing away in this newsroom since 1980. I have always said that I have the best job in the world, and I continue to think I totally lucked out when executive editor Buzz Merritt and managing editor Joe Harper insisted I come to work here.

The late Diane Lewis sealed the deal, and I stumbled off the elevator one Monday morning not knowing straight up from sic 'em. It was going to be on-the-job learning for sure. Jon Roe was given the task of teaching me how to write. How lucky was I to get to learn from such a superb writer! I still hear his voice when I'm writing. And I must say that he's the one who convinced me I could do this job. "Just write the way you talk. Use your voice," he would say when my writing was stilted, contrived — and who knows what else.

After much prodding, I decided to just "talk" to the readers. As a former junior high physical education teacher, then an assistant athletic director in women's athletics, it took a long time before I could say, "I am a writer" and believe it.

Fran Kentling, who quickly became a dear friend, encouraged me and continually gave me good advice. The job I decided to try for a year turned into two years, then three. And now it's more than three decades later. There have been very few days when I wanted to jump off the roof, slam the phone down or hide under my desk — as if that would be possible with all the junk I have under there.

It's been interesting how many people have suggested other jobs I should do after leaving *The Eagle*. They suggest another company to work for or another career to take up. No, no. If I wanted to work, I'd stay right here. People have asked what I'm going to do to stay busy. Actually, I don't want to be busy. I love the volunteer work I do in our community, and I'm not retiring from that. But I'm looking forward to a slower pace with a lot fewer deadlines. It seems I can't figure out any other way to slow down.

In the past year, there have been too many days of feeling a bit overwhelmed. I'm not spending enough time with the very important people in my life. It's time to quit scheduling every hour of every day. I'm not complaining one bit because I know how lucky I've been to look forward to going to work. And I'm thankful every day that I love my life. There's just so much of it. And that's a good thing. More on all this later.

My last day isn't until June 28, so don't stop reading! It's going to be fun to take a look back when I have time.

This job in a word: opportunities
June 18, 2012

The question has been asked many times in the past few weeks: "Aren't you going to miss your job when you retire?" The answer? Yes. Working for *The Eagle* has given me the opportunity to meet people famous and infamous. And I've had many experiences I wouldn't have otherwise had if I'd continued teaching physical education or working as the assistant to the director in women's athletics at Wichita State University.

Where else would you get the opportunity to play Gumby and tackle The Famous San Diego Chicken at a Wichita Wranglers baseball game? Yes, I did that. Just so you know, a foam rubber

Gumby costume makes it difficult to run, and it's hot. Really, really hot.

The same editor sent me to Valley Center to meet the train that brought the circus to town. I rode an elephant from Valley Center to the Kansas Coliseum. That might not seem very far, but an elephant is slow going. And no, I wasn't waving from a comfortable basket balanced on Julia's back. I was astride that elephant. When I got down — with the help of the very handsome animal trainer — I could barely walk. I also had the adventure of rappelling down the side of the 14-story Ambassador Hotel. I volunteered for that, it wasn't assigned.

Needless to say, it's also been fun to meet famous people. Going to Fashion Week in New York gave me the opportunity to chat with a lot of stars. Almost without exception, they were very nice. Debra Messing, Cheryl Hines, Carol Burnett, Ana Ortiz and Kelly Pickler were really fun. OK, since I'm name dropping, here are some others I've met in the past 32 years: Monty Hall, Esther Williams, Richard Simmons, Tammy Faye Baker, Carol Alt, Dick Clark, Bernadette Peters, Beverly Sills, Mary Wilson of the Supremes, Martin Sheen, and Martin Short.

I had brief but fun meetings with Kelly Ripa, Randy Jackson, Regis Philbin, Ivana Trump, Tommay Lasorda, Harrison Ford, Craig Ferguson and Sean Combs.

I'll never forget my first interview with a star, Patricia Neal. I was so nervous I thought I'd faint. We talked for two hours. Then she sent me a postcard and later a letter! Jon Roe said, "Don't think this will always happen. Most of the time you won't hear anything after a story runs." He was right.

But I've always been even more thrilled to talk to famous fashion designers. Jewelry designer David Yurman is my all-time favorite. But I was beside myself when I got to interview Hubert de Givenchy and Gianni Versace. I was able to speak briefly to Oscar de la Renta, and I will never forget the first time I got a few quotes from Ralph Lauren.

All right, enough of this reminiscing.

But one more thing. I got to do the pre-performance phone interview with Jerry Seinfeld when he came to do a benefit show after the tornado in Andover. We talked about "Seinfeld," why he was coming, etc. and before we hung up, he said, "You're funny, Bonnie." I could have died happy that minute: Jerry Seinfeld said I was funny! Wow, talk to Jerry Seinfeld and get paid for it. Good job to have. And yes, I'll miss it.

Bonnie after rappelling down the Ambassador Hotel

Bonnie in retirement

Acknowledgments

If I'm honest with you I rarely read the acknowledgments at the end of a book. I've wondered why the author bothers with all the names of people we don't know.

Now I understand. I wouldn't want this book to go to press without being able to publicly thank the many people who helped me get this book finished and published. Let me tell you, publishing a book is a whole lot harder than writing a column and sending it to an editor.

I had the help of people I respect and now owe each of them a huge debt of gratitude. At the top of the list is Lisa Corbin who was with me every step of the way. There would not be a book without her insistence and assistance.

A big thanks to editor Gretchen Eick at Blue Cedar Press. She answered many, many questions and gave sound advice to us. Lisa and I needed it because we knew nothing, and I mean *nothing* about putting a book together. Gretchen is one patient woman.

The cover art was done by the very talented Richard Crowson. The also very talented Rod Pocowatchit was on vacation but found time to work on the cover design. Thanks guys.

Thanks to those who were willing to write blurbs: Bob Getz, Carrie Rengers, Tom Shine, Suzanne Perez, Jean Hays, Annie Garvey, Ruthie Williams and Mark McCormick. And to Denise Neil for writing the Forward.

And thank you to Michael Roehrman, editor of Kansas.com and *The Wichita Eagle*, for giving me permission to do this book. He also is the person I send my columns to now. I could not ask to work with a nicer, more patient person.

Barbara Withrow voluntarily edited this book. Not only is she an excellent editor, she's a wonderful friend.

Stacey Stamps came to the rescue with expert technical assistance. It was much needed. Bless her heart! I marveled at how easily she made it all work in a matter of one hour.

Thanks to my very supportive family. Daughter, Susan Honeyman, has said for years I should do this book. A professor at the University of Nebraska, Kearney, she has written several books and seems to always be working on the next one. After this experience I admire her even more.

Son, Marshall, his wife Michele, and all the grandkids, who with their fun personalities and life experiences, give me lots of ideas for columns. And love.

Last, but certainly not least, a big fat kiss and thank you to my husband, Dick Honeyman. He never complained even though he didn't have a home cooked meal or much attention from me for at least a month. I'm so appreciative of his encouragement, moral support, editing suggestions and trips to pick up take-out food. He did, however, ask a number of times when the book would be finished.

And thank *you* for being a reader. It is much appreciated. And keep in touch...

Bonnie Bing
bingbylines@gmail.com

Young Bonnie

Bonnie and her husband Dick Honeyman at his birthday

Bonnie as the Gridiron fairy princess

Bonnie in the newsroom of *The Wichita Eagle*